Nelson Thornes **Framework English**

Access

Skills in **Non-Fiction**

Wendy Wren

Series Consultant:
John Jackman

Scottish Consultant:
Sandra Ferguson

Nelson Thornes

Contents

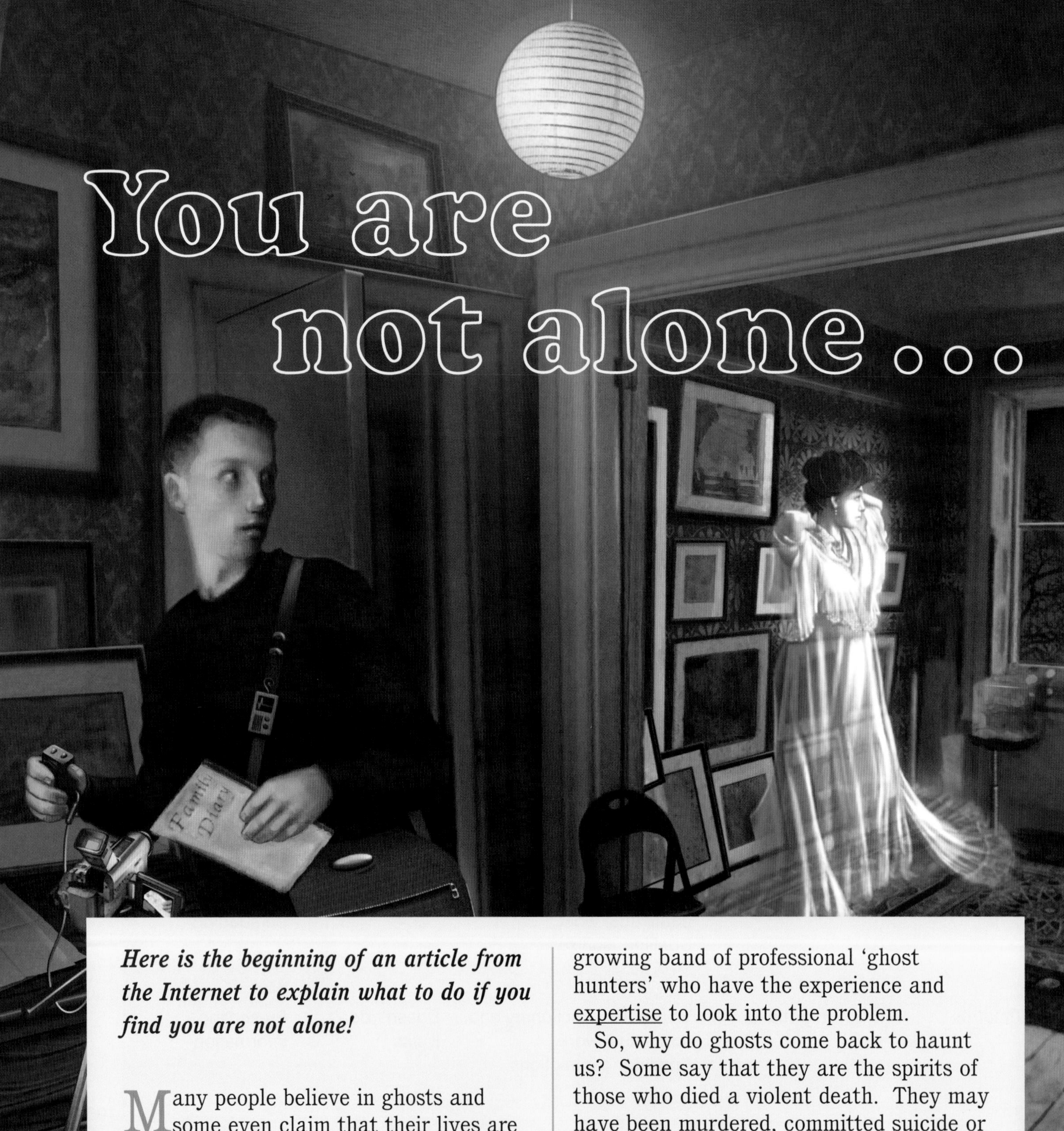

You are not alone ...

Here is the beginning of an article from the Internet to explain what to do if you find you are not alone!

Many people believe in ghosts and some even claim that their lives are being made a misery by their unwelcome visitors. But help is at hand as there is a growing band of professional 'ghost hunters' who have the experience and expertise to look into the problem.

So, why do ghosts come back to haunt us? Some say that they are the spirits of those who died a violent death. They may have been murdered, committed suicide or suffered a tragic accident. Others believe that the ghost returns to a place in which they spent a lot of time during their life. It might be their house, or a church or pub. If the particular building has been changed in some way, the ghost may appear to walk through a wall where there was once a door, or float in the air where there was once a staircase.

It must be remembered that ghosts do not intend harm to the living. People may be so frightened that they fall and hurt themselves in an attempt to escape, but a ghost itself will not cause physical injury. However, many people refuse to live with these unwelcome apparitions and the ghost hunters are called in.

The first contact is usually by phone, and the ghost hunter will ask for a name and address, religion, marital status, number of children in the family and their ages. It is then important to find out some information about the ghost. When was the ghost first seen? Does it haunt particular rooms in the house and at what times of day? Are there musical sounds or the movement of objects? One very important question is that of witnesses. How many people have seen the ghost? If it is only one person then the ghost hunter has to consider the possibility of nightmares or the use of drugs or alcohol. All this information helps the ghost hunter to decide if the ghost is a poltergeist, a haunting or the result of something more normal. It is also important for the ghost hunter to find out if the family are under unusual stress at home or at work. If other investigators have been involved it will be useful to speak to them.

Finally, the ghost hunters have to be clear on what they are being asked to do. Not everyone is looking for the ghost to be removed! Some are just curious to find out why they have been singled out to be haunted.

Once the telephone conversation has ended, the ghost hunter will gather his or her team together and a visit will be made to the haunted property. The other members of the team are told very little so they do not make any snap judgements. They are there to investigate and collect data and make sure that there is no simple explanation for the 'haunting'. If all else fails, a psychic may be called in to find out exactly what is going on.

COMPREHENSION

A Copy these sentences. Fill in the missing words.

1. Ghosts may be the spirits of those who died a _ _ _ _ _ _ _ _ death.
2. Ghosts do not intend to _ _ _ _ the living.
3. A ghost hunter needs to know how many _ _ _ _ _ _ have seen the ghost.
4. Not everyone is looking for the ghost to be _ _ _ _ _ _ _.
5. If all else fails, a _ _ _ _ _ _ _ may be called in.

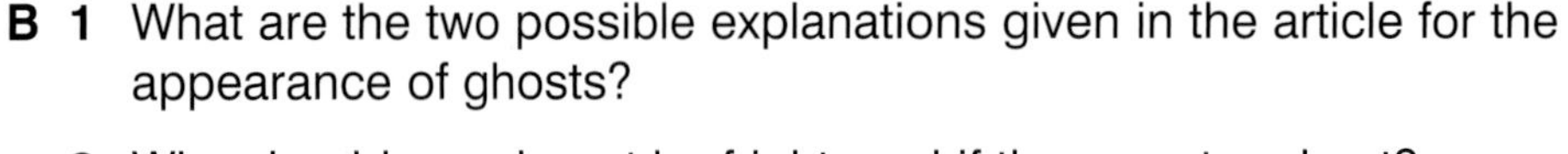

B **1** What are the two possible explanations given in the article for the appearance of ghosts?

2 Why should people not be frightened if they meet a ghost?

3 Why does the ghost hunter not share all the information with the team?

4 Why do you think it is important for the ghost hunter to know if '*the family are under unusual stress at home or at work*'?

5 Why do you think it is important that the ghost hunter knows how many people have seen the ghost?

C **1** For what purpose do you think the author has written this article?

2 Who do you think might be interested to read it?

VOCABULARY

Use a dictionary and the context of the passage to explain the meanings of the following words. They are underlined in the passage. The first one is done for you.

1 expertise = skill **2** tragic **3** physical

4 poltergeist **5** data **6** psychic

SPELLING

Root words and derivations

The English language we speak today is made up of many words which have been *derived* (come from) other languages. Over the centuries, we have been invaded by the Romans, by German tribes and by the French. Many of their words, in some form, are part of our language today.

Copy these words:

poltergeist investigate research initial

Match each word you have copied with a root word in the box. The first one is done for you.

poltergeist = poltern

Word	Language	Meaning
vestigare	Latin	to track
initialis	Latin	beginning
poltern	German	to create a disturbance
recherche	French	to search

GRAMMAR AND PUNCTUATION

Verbs

Verbs are usually 'action' words,
eg *'Does it **haunt** particular rooms ...'*
A verb can also be a 'being' word,
eg *'they **are** the spirits ...'*
Verbs come in families. The family name is called the **infinitive** and begins, with 'to',
eg *to haunt* *to be*

A Write the infinitives of the underlined verbs. The first one is done for you.

1. Some people suffer tragic accidents. *infinitive = to suffer*
2. A building may have been changed in some way.
3. A ghost will not cause physical injury.

The members of a verb family are the different tenses of a verb.

Present tense	**Past tense**	**Future tense**
What is happening, eg *it haunts*	What has happened, eg *it haunted*	What will happen, eg *it will haunt*

B Change these present tense sentences into the past tense. The first one is done for you.

1. People often fear ghosts. *People often feared ghosts.*
2. The ghost hunter asks many questions.
3. A team visits the haunted building

HINT
Tense means time.

The words *am was have has will* are **auxiliary** verbs.
They help you to know the **tense** of a verb.

C Copy these sentences. Underline the auxiliary verb and say what the tense is. The first one is done for you.

1. He has seen a ghost. *He has seen a ghost. past*
2. People will contact ghost hunters by telephone.
3. People have believed in ghosts for centuries.

HINT
Auxiliary verbs are sometimes called 'helper' verbs.

Family
Diary

WRITING

Explanations

Ghost hunting is a piece of non-fiction writing.
Its purpose is **to explain** the job of the ghost hunter.

Language features

Introduction

The first paragraph of an explanation should make it clear what you are explaining. In the first paragraph of *Ghost hunting* we learn that:

- people believe in ghosts
- people are haunted by ghosts
- ghost hunters can help.

Paragraphing

Explanations must be written step-by-step. To make sure the explanation is not muddled, you should make a paragraph plan. In *Ghost hunting*, the writer has organised the first few paragraphs like this:

Paragraph	Content
1	Introduces what is to be explained
2	Explains why ghosts haunt and where they haunt
3	Explains that ghosts are not harmful

Present tense

Explanations are usually written in the present tense, eg

'Many people believe in ghosts ...', *'The first contact is usually by phone ...'*

Writing assignment

After the first visit to the haunted property, the ghost hunter still has more work to do. These are the next steps.

Step 1 The ghost hunter asks the haunted family to keep a diary. They should write down the times, dates and places where the ghost is seen.

Step 2 A second visit to the house is made with equipment such as cameras, tape recorders and camcorders.

Write the next two paragraphs of the explanation using the information in 1 and 2.

- Write mostly in the present tense.
- Try to think of reasons why the ghost hunter would do these things.

They were not alone . . .

In his book 'My Solitary Life', *Augustus Hare recounts the strange tale of Croglin Grange. Two brothers and a sister moved into the large house in Cumberland only to find that they were not alone.*

One night, shortly after they had moved into the Grange, the sister found it impossible to sleep. She got up and looked out of her window and was surprised to see two lights flickering in the trees. The lights came towards her and she realised they were eyes, blazing in the face of *something horrible*. Every moment it was coming nearer and nearer. She was horrified and tried to scream but she could make no sound.

She ran to her bedroom door to unlock it but, at that moment, she heard a scratching sound at the window. She turned to see a hideous brown face with flaming eyes staring in at her. The creature broke the window and entered the room. She couldn't move as it came towards her, twisted her hair with its bony finger and bit her in the throat.

At last she was able to scream and her brothers broke down the door. By the time they got inside, the creature had escaped through the window and their sister was unconscious on the floor. One brother chased the monster but it climbed over the churchyard wall and disappeared.

The doctor was called and it was decided that she should go to Switzerland to recover from the frightening experience. She was soon well enough to return home convinced that the 'monster' had been an escaped lunatic who had probably been caught and would not be visiting them again. Back at Croglin Grange, she kept her shutters locked at night and her brothers slept with loaded pistols in their rooms.

A few peaceful months passed before the sister was awakened by the same scratching noise at her window. Through the pane at the top which the shutters did not cover, she saw the same hideous face! This time she screamed at once and her brothers came rushing in, pistols at the ready. As the creature ran away, one brother fired and hit it in the leg. Once again it scrambled over the churchyard wall and into an old burial vault.

The next day they went inside the vault. All of the coffins except one were opened and the bones scattered on the floor. Inside the undisturbed coffin they found the hideous creature who had appeared at the window, with a bullet wound in its leg. The coffin and its contents were immediately burnt, which is the only way to get rid of a vampire!

Based on *My Solitary Life* by Augustus Hare

COMPREHENSION

A Write 'true' or 'false' for each of these statements.

1. The sister saw two lights flickering in the trees.
2. The creature came in through the window.
3. One of her brothers caught the monster.
4. When the creature came a second time, the brothers attacked it with swords.
5. Burning is the only way to get rid of a vampire.

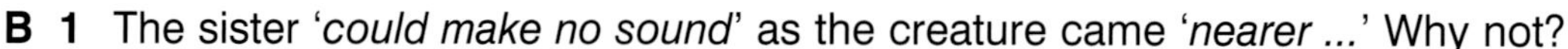

B **1** The sister '*could make no sound*' as the creature came '*nearer ...*' Why not?

2 In the second paragraph, what makes you think the creature is a vampire?

3 After returning from Switzerland, how did they protect themselves?

4 Why did the creature not enter the sister's bedroom on the second visit?

5 Why was everyone so sure that the '*hideous creature*' in the coffin was the same '*hideous creature*' at the window?

C **1** For what purpose do you think the writer has recounted this story?

2 Who do you think might be interested to read it?

VOCABULARY

Use a dictionary and the context of the passage to explain the meaning of these words. They are underlined in the passage. The first one is done for you.

1 horrified = terrified	**2** hideous	**3** unconscious
4 convinced	**5** vault	**6** undisturbed

SPELLING

Vowel sounds

HINT

*A long vowel sound is the **name** of the vowel.*

Vowels can make a **short** sound,

eg **a** as in *had*, **e** as in *leg*, **i** as in *bit*, **o** as in *top*, **u** as in *but*

Vowels can also make a **long** sound,

eg		
a + e as in *came*	**ai** as in *again*	**ay** as in *away*
ea as in *scream*	**ee** as in *sleep*	
i + e as in *time*	**ight** as in *night*	
o + e as in *broke*	**oa** as in *throat*	**ow** as in *window*
u + e as in *huge*	**ue** as in *due*	**ew** as in *few*

Copy the words below. Underline the vowel sound, write S for short or L for long.

The first one is done for you.

1 had = h<u>a</u>d S	**2** got	**3** light
4 tree	**5** face	**6** size
7 chase	**8** home	**9** rush
10 each	**11** threw	**12** roast

GRAMMAR AND PUNCTUATION

Adverbs

Adverbs tell us more about verbs.
Adverbs tells us:

- how something happens, eg *scream* ***loudly***
  verb adverb
- when something happens, eg *scream* ***before***
  verb adverb
- where something happens, eg *scream* ***outside***
  verb adverb

A Copy the headings below.

How **When** **Where**

Put each of the adverbs in the box under the correct heading.

soon slowly today here seriously mildly
afterwards happily far suddenly securely
now outside quickly above there

Adverbs can also tell us more about adjectives,

eg *She was **slightly** red in the face.*
adverb adjective

*She was **very** red in the face.*
adverb adjective

'**Slightly** red' is different from '**very** red'.

B Choose the correct answer.

1. If you were **very** scared would you be **quite** scared or **extremely** scared?
2. If you were **very** annoyed would you be **slightly** annoyed or **terribly** annoyed?
3. If you were **very** bored would you be **hardly** bored or **thoroughly** bored?

C Use these adverb + adjectives phrases in sentences of your own.

1 barely awake
2 utterly exhausted
3 greatly troubled
4 faintly surprised

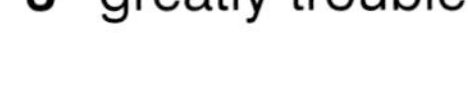

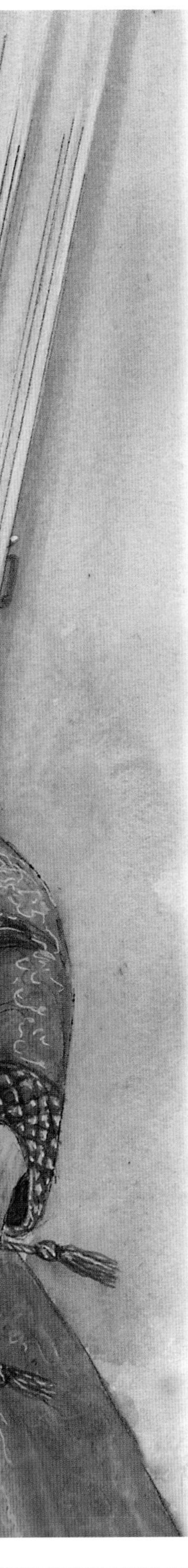

WRITING

Recount

In his book *My Solitary Life*, Augustus Hare tells us what happened at Croglin Grange. This style of writing is called a **recount**.

- The writer gives the facts of the story.
- He does not say whether he believes the story or not.

Language features

Viewpoint

The writer was not at Croglin Grange when all this happened so he writes in the third person,

eg *'... **they** had moved into the Grange ...'*, *'**She** got up ...'*

If someone was recounting something that had happened to them, he or she would use the first person,

eg *... **we** had moved into the Grange ..., **I** got up ...*

Past tense

A recount tells us about something that has already happened. It is written in the past tense,

eg *'The creature **broke** the window ...'*, *'... the sister **was awakened** ...'*

Paragraphing

A recount tells us about what has happened in the order in which it happened. The paragraphs often begin with 'time-phrases' so we can tell when things happened,

eg *'One night ...'*
'At last ...'
'A few peaceful months passed ...'
'The next day ...'

Writing assignment

Imagine you are one of the brothers in the story. Recount what happened at Croglin Grange from your point of view. Remember to:

- write in the first person
- use the past tense
- recount what happened in the correct order
- use time phrases to begin your paragraphs.

Think carefully about what **you** saw and did, **not** what your sister saw and did!

That's amazing...

1 England's unpopular King John, who reigned from 1199 to 1216, was said to have been a werewolf. The legend tells how monks, hearing sounds from his grave, dug him up and took his body out of consecrated ground.

2 In 16th-century Italy, it was believed that some werewolves grew hair on the inside of their body. In 1541, at least one suspect died while being cut open to see if this was true!

3 There have been odd cases of people who believed they were animals. They tried to drink blood and eat raw flesh.

4 There is a rare disease which causes a fur-like growth on people's skin. It is easy to see how such people would be feared and cast out from their community.

5 The name 'werewolf' could have come from the Old English 'wer' which means 'man', so we get 'werewolf'.

There are many werewolf legends which probably come from the myths of the Norse gods. These gods were said to change into animal forms, such as the bear and the wolf. During the 16th-century witch-hunts, it was believed that a witch could change into a wolf as well as such animals as toads, cats and hares.

As humans, werewolves and vampires look alike. They have eyebrows which meet in the middle, small, pointed ears, claw-like fingernails and hair growing on the palms. But there is one slight difference: a werewolf's third finger on each hand is supposed to be as long as, or longer than, the second finger.

When a human changes into a werewolf, it can appear as an extra large wolf which moves on all fours, or as a hairy biped, with horrible features and clawed hands. In either of these shapes, it tears out the throats of its animal or human victims and then devours the flesh raw.

How do you become a werewolf?

There are many ways in which a person might become a werewolf. Stripping naked and rolling in the sand under a full moon was thought to be one way. Being conceived at the time of a new moon or simply sleeping outdoors under a full moon on a Friday is enough to create a werewolf.

In Ireland, St Patrick is said to have cursed a whole clan who displeased him by their lack of faith. As a result they turned into werewolves every seven years.

Some European legends say that drinking from a stream from which a wolf has drunk, being bitten by a rabid wolf or simply eating the wolfbane plant will cause the transformation.

How do you deal with werewolves?

There are many ways in which werewolves can be got rid of. Some people say that speaking the name of Christ, or calling the werewolf three times by his true Christian name can set a person free from the werewolf's spirit.

In France, it was said that the werewolf could be defeated by taking three drops of blood from the creature during its wolf period.

By far the best known method of freeing a human from the curse of the werewolf is to shoot the creature with a silver bullet, preferably made of consecrated silver, such as a crucifix from a church.

Based on *Strange Stories Amazing Facts*, Reader's Digest

COMPREHENSION

A Choose the best answer for each question.

1. Norse gods were said to change into:
   a vampires **b** animals **c** witches.
2. Werewolves have hair growing:
   a in their ears **b** in their fingernails **c** on their palms.
3. When a human changes into a werewolf it can look like:
   a a big wolf **b** King John **c** St Patrick.
4. People can become werewolves by sleeping:
   a under a full moon **b** in the sand **c** only on Friday.
5. You can get rid of a werewolf by:
   a drinking its blood **b** shooting it with a bullet **c** taking it to church.

B 1 Explain in your own words, '*the myths of the Norse gods*'.

2 How many ways of becoming a werewolf can you find in the article?

3 How many ways of getting rid of werewolves can you find in the article?

4 How does the writer think the name 'werewolf' may have come about?

5 Explain why you think the writer either:
a believes in werewolves **b** does not believe in werewolves.

C 1 List the ways in which information about werewolves is presented.

2 Where do you think you would find a piece of writing like this?

VOCABULARY

Use a dictionary and the context of the article to explain the meanings of these words. They are underlined in the passage. The first one is done for you.

1 biped = two-footed animal **2** devours **3** clan

4 rabid **5** transformation **6** consecrated

SPELLING

The 'oo' sound

The letters **oo** make two different sounds:

- a short sound, eg *foot* (sounds like p**u**t)
- a long sound, eg *moon* (sounds like t**une**)

A Write each word from the box under the correct heading.

oo = short sound oo = long sound

food good poor book wood scoop hook hood

The letters **ou** can make three different sounds:

- gr**ou**p (like sc**oo**p) • fam**ou**s (like f**u**ss) • h**ou**nd (like t**ow**n)

B Write each word from the box under the correct heading.

ou as in group ou as in famous ou as in hound

south dangerous pouch could round cloud
mouth spout scrounge good enormous
about religious mouse should

GRAMMAR AND PUNCTUATION

Pronouns

A **pronoun** is a word that can be used instead of a noun,
eg *A vampire has pointed ears.* (A vampire – noun)
It has pointed ears. (It – pronoun)

A Read the sentences. Write the pronouns from the box you could use instead of the underlined words. The first one is done for you.

they he it we them

HINT
Remember! A noun is a naming word.

1 King John reigned from 1199 to 1216. He
2 A werewolf has eyebrows which meet in the middle.
3 The monks dug up King John's grave.
4 St Patrick cursed a whole clan.
5 You can get rid of werewolves in many ways.
6 My friends and I do not believe in werewolves.

Some **pronouns** tell us 'who owns something',
eg *The body they dug up was* ***King John's body****.*
The body they dug up was **his**.

B Read the sentences. Write the pronoun from the box you could use instead of the underlined words. The first one is done for you.

his theirs hers mine

HINT
These are called possessive pronouns.

1 The book on werewolves is my book. mine
2 The curse that turned the clan into werewolves was St Patrick's curse.
3 The werewolf costumes are my brothers'.
4 The video of the werewolf film is my sister's.

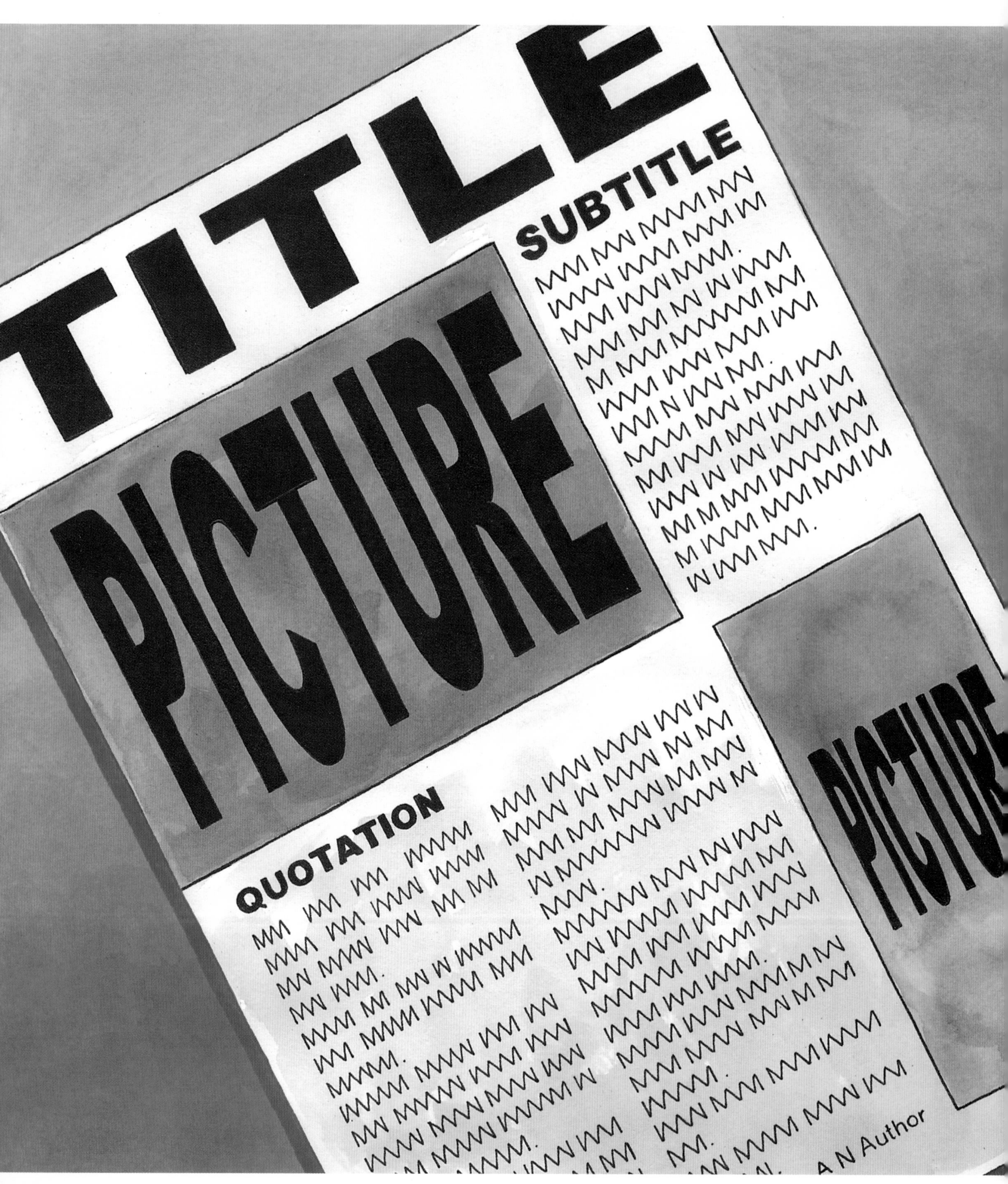
TITLE
SUBTITLE
PICTURE
QUOTATION
PICTURE
A N Author

WRITING

Magazine articles

Magazine articles are usually written to:

- inform ie, they should give you information
- entertain ie, they should be interesting and enjoyable.

Some magazines are all about one subject, eg *Football Focus.*

Other magazines have articles on lots of different subjects.

Language features

Main heading

The main heading or title of the article must grab your attention!
The writer has used: *Big bad werewolves.*

'**B**ig **b**ad' is alliteration. This is when words begin with the same sound.

Can you think of another title for the article which uses alliteration?

Introduction

The first few paragraphs of the article should let you know what it is about:

'There are many werewolf legends ...'

Sub-headings

These are smaller headings used in the article to let you know what the next bit is going to be about, eg *How do you become a werewolf?*

Using questions as sub-headings is a good idea because you want to read on to find the answers!

Layout

A whole page of writing doesn't look very interesting. It might put you off!
The writer has made '*Big bad werewolves*' look interesting by using:

- sub-headings
- pictures
- information boxes.

Writing assignment

Choose something you are interested in and write an article for a magazine.
You will need to:

- think of a title that will grab the reader's attention
- make notes on the information you find
- use sub-headings and boxed information
- do a rough plan so that you know where the writing and the pictures will go.

I have
a dream ...

Martin Luther King was born on 15 January 1929 in Atlanta, Georgia. He was ordained as a Baptist minister in 1948. He became a very important man in the civil rights movement which wanted black people to be treated in the same way as white people. On 28 August 1963 he gave his most famous speech which began 'I have a dream' and 250,000 people gathered to listen.

I have a dream that one day this nation will rise up and live out the true meaning of its creed: 'We hold these truths to be self-evident: that all men are created equal.' I have a dream that one day on the red hills of Georgia the sons of former slaves and the sons of former slaveowners will be able to sit down together at a table of brotherhood ... I have a dream that my four children will one day live in a nation where they will not be judged by the colour of their skin but by the content of their character. I have a dream today.

I have a dream that one day the state of Alabama ... little black boys and black girls will be able to join hands with little white boys and white girls and walk together as sisters and brothers. I have a dream today ... With this faith we will be able to work together, to pray together, to struggle together, to go to jail together, to stand up for freedom together, knowing that we will be free one day.

This will be the day when all of God's children will be able to sing with a new meaning, 'My country, 'tis of thee, sweet land of liberty, of thee I sing. Land where my fathers died, land of the pilgrim's pride, from every mountainside, let freedom ring.' And if America is to be a great nation, this must become true ... From every mountainside, let freedom ring.

When we let freedom ring, when we let it ring from every village and every hamlet, from every state and every city, we will be able to speed up that day when all of God's children, black men and white men, Jews and Gentiles, Protestants and Catholics, will be able to join hands and sing in the words of the old Negro spiritual, 'Free at last! Free at last! Thank God Almighty, we are free at last!'

COMPREHENSION

A Copy these sentences. Fill in the missing words.

1. Martin Luther King believed that all men are created _ _ _ _ _.
2. People should not be judged by the colour of their _ _ _ _.
3. People should be judged by the content of their _ _ _ _ _ _ _ _ _.
4. America will be a great _ _ _ _ _ _ when all of its people are free.
5. He wants _ _ _ _ _ _ _ to ring from every mountainside.

B **1** What evidence can you find in the speech which shows that Americans once owned slaves?

2 What does Martin Luther King hope for his four children?

3 What do you think Martin Luther King means when he says he wants white and black children to '*walk together as sisters and brothers*'?

4 Why do you think the people he is speaking to might have to '*go to jail*'?

5 How do you know that Martin Luther King wants everyone to be free, not just the black people?

C Explain in your own words what Martin Luther King's dream was.

VOCABULARY

Use a dictionary and the context of the speech to explain the meanings of these words. They are underlined in the passage. The first one is done for you.

1 creed = *beliefs* **2** brotherhood **3** liberty

4 hamlet **5** Gentiles **6** Negro spiritual

SPELLING

Prefixes

A **prefix** is a group of letters put at the beginning of a word to change its meaning,

eg visit ***re**visit*

Many prefixes change a word into its opposite,

eg true ***un**true*

Use the prefixes in the box to make these words into their opposites. The first one is done for you.

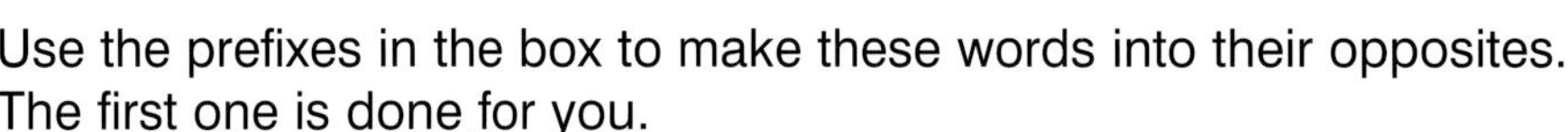

1 equal = *unequal* **2** able **3** happy

4 known **5** mortal **6** sure

7 pleasant **8** possible **9** appear

HINT

Remember the rule with prefixes – just add them!

GRAMMAR AND PUNCTUATION

Sentences

All sentences:
- make sense
- begin with a capital letter
- end with a full stop, a question mark or an exclamation mark.

A Copy these sentences and add the correct punctuation. The first one is done for you.

1 we make dreams come true *We make dreams come true!*
2 freedom is needed now
3 which side are you on
4 everyone should have a dream
5 it is just not fair

A **simple sentence**:
- makes sense
- is a complete thought
- is one main clause.

B Not all of these are sentences. Write the numbers of the complete sentences.

1 Martin Luther King spoke about.
2 He had a dream.
3 Martin Luther King's four children.
4 America will be a great nation.
5 Thank God we are.

C Finish the incomplete sentences.

WRITING

Writing to persuade

When Martin Luther King wrote his '*I have a dream*' speech, he was trying to **persuade** his listeners that all people should be treated in the same way. It should not matter about the colour of their skin, their nationality or their religion.

Language features

Facts

To persuade people that you know what you are writing or talking about, it is a good idea to include facts.

- Martin Luther King knows the states which owned slaves and he names some of them:

  '*Georgia*' '*Alabama*'
- He knows the American constitution (laws) and he uses part of it in his speech:

  '*all men are created equal*'

Repetition

Repeating important words and phrases make them stick in the mind of your reader or listener. Count how many times Martin Luther King uses these words:

- dream
- freedom
- free.

Vivid language

You should use vivid words and phrases to show how strongly you feel. Martin Luther King:

- wants to '*let freedom ring*'
- is willing to '*struggle*'; '*go to jail*' and '*stand up for freedom*'.

Writing assignment

Write a persuasive speech you can deliver to your class.

- Choose a subject you feel strongly about.
- Research your subject so you can include some facts.
- Repeat important words and phrases so they will stick in the minds of your listeners.
- Use vivid language to show your audience how strongly you feel.

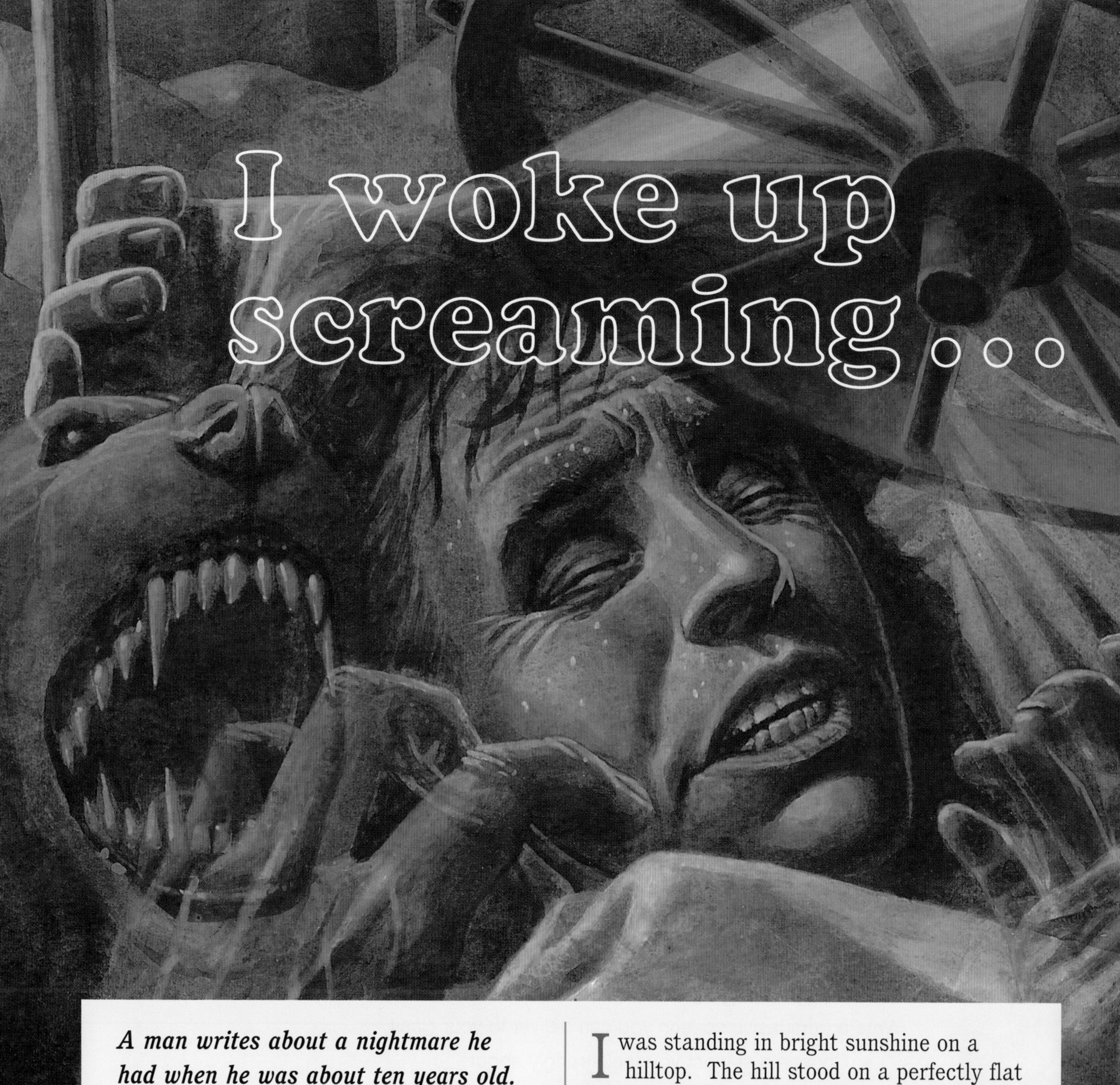

I woke up screaming . . .

A man writes about a nightmare he had when he was about ten years old. He woke screaming and had to be calmed by parents.

I was standing in bright sunshine on a hilltop. The hill stood on a perfectly flat plain. The hill was covered in bright green grass. The sky above was a crisp, clean blue, with a few clouds dotted about.

I stood with arms outstretched, slowly turning round and round. As I turned, I hummed quietly and contentedly. Below me the patchwork patterns of fields circled, creating the feeling of a fairground ride.

Suddenly, there was a movement of a shadow on the ground. There was something behind me. I glanced over my shoulder in fear. What I saw made me want to scream but I couldn't. There was a huge wheel with spokes as bright as spears, rolling towards me.

I tried to scurry away round the side of the wheel but to my horror, as I scampered, it turned towards me. It just kept coming towards me!

I began to struggle backwards, down the slope, on my backside. My one thought was to escape this wheel. But it just kept coming! I spun around and lurched to my feet. Staggering, I headed down the hillside, the wheel rolling after me.

Turning again, I saw that the wheel seemed to rise and rise into the sky. My head strained backwards as I tried to see the top of the wheel. The wheel loomed over me and then seemed to swoop down on me.

In panic, I spun around and fled. My arms were stretched out from my sides, like wings or sails, as if I could escape by flying away. Behind me the wheel began to gather speed. As I ran, I glanced first over one shoulder, then over the other. No matter how fast I ran, the wheel was gaining on me. I ran. My lungs were aching. My heart pumped frantically in my ears. My legs thudded on the turf. My knees threatened to give way: muscles, tendons and ligaments snapping like rubber bands.

As exhaustion overtook me, my stride faltered. I felt in danger of being overrun by the wheels as it hurtled down the hill. Suddenly, I felt the rim of the wheel touch my back.

Still, I could not cry or scream. My breaths were short sobbing gasps of air, sucked in desperately. It was no good, I could not breathe, I could not cry, I could not outrun the wheel. My fate was sealed; there was no way out. I was going to be overtaken. I would be crushed by the enormous wheel!

I fell headlong. I tucked and I rolled, whirling over and over. With a thud, the air was blasted from my lungs. The wheel came on and rolled over me. I screamed at last!

Then the light dazzled me. My father put his arm around my shuddering shoulders and said, 'Wake up, son. It's all right. Was it the same dream again?'

COMPREHENSION

A Write 'true' or 'false' for each statement.

1. The writer was at the top of a hill.
2. He turned and saw a huge wheel.
3. The wheel rolled by him.
4. He escaped the wheel by flying.
5. He screamed only when the wheel rolled over him.

B 1 Before the wheel appeared, how do you think the writer was feeling?

2 Why do you think the writer couldn't scream?

3 Find three examples which show what was happening to the writer's body as he ran faster and faster.

4 What do you think he means when he says, '*my fate was sealed*'?

5 How do you know that the writer had had the dream before?

C Sometimes nightmares are caused by something that has happened to us or that we have seen when we are awake. What do you think might have caused this nightmare?

VOCABULARY

Use a dictionary and the context of the passage to explain the meaning of these words. They are underlined in the passage. The first one is done for you.

1 contentedly = happily	**2** lurched	**3** frantically
4 faltered	**5** hurtled	**6** headlong

SPELLING

Prefixes

Remember! A **prefix** is a group of letters put at the beginning of a word to change its meaning. If the last letter of the prefix and the first letter of the word are the same, you will have a double letter in the new word,

eg over + run = *overrun*

A Choose a prefix from the box to add to each word. All the new words you make will have a double letter. The first one is done for you.

over dis un im il

1 similar = dissimilar	**2** natural	**3** modest
4 legal	**5** rule	**6** legible
7 service	**8** movable	**9** named

HINT

The spelling rule is easy. Just add it!

B Choose five of the new words you have made and use them in sentences of your own.

GRAMMAR AND PUNCTUATION

Sentence types

A **sentence** is a group of words which make sense.

sentence: I had an awful nightmare.
non-sentence: The nightmare was about.

There are three main types of sentences:

- statements: tell us something; end with a full stop **.**
- questions: ask us something; end with a question mark **?**
- exclamations: show fear, anger, surprise, etc.; end with an exclamation mark **!**

A Copy these sentences. Add the correct punctuation.

1. The grass was bright green and the sky was blue
2. What was causing the shadow
3. I was horrified
4. Would the wheel crush me to death
5. I woke up screaming

When **statements** become **questions**:

- the order of the words change,
  eg statement: ***There was** a huge wheel*.
  question: ***Was there** a huge wheel*?
- words may be added or changed,
  eg statement: ***I wanted** to escape*.
  question: ***Did you want** to escape*?

B Change these statements into questions. The first one is done for you.

1. I glanced over my shoulder. *Did you glance over your shoulder?*
2. There was no way to escape.
3. The wheel loomed over me.
4. The rim of the wheel touched my back.
5. It was the same dream again.

WRITING

Recount

In this **recount**, the writer tells us what is happening to him. This is his nightmare so he writes in the first person.

Language features

Writing in the first person

Writing about something that has happened to you can be very boring if you begin every sentence with 'I'. Think about:

- changing the order of the words,
  eg I spun round in panic. ⟶ *In panic, I spun round ...*
- using conjunctions to join sentences,
  eg I spun around. I lurched to my feet.
  ⟶ *I spun around and lurched to my feet.*

Writing in the past tense

When you recount something, use the past tense. What you are recounting has already happened,

eg *'I was standing ...'* *'I glanced ...'* *'My head strained ...'*

Ordering paragraphs

Write the events in the order in which they happened. This helps the reader to understand exactly what happened to you.

Vocabulary choices

When something has happened to you, you have certain feelings about it. You may look back with pleasure or fear or anger. The words you choose in your recount will let the reader know how you feel. Find five words or phrases in the passage which let you know that the writer is very, very frightened.

Writing assignment

Recount an experience you have had. It might be a nightmare or it could be something very pleasant. Remember to:

- write in the first person but don't begin every sentence with 'I'
- recount what happened in the correct order
- write in the past tense
- choose your words carefully so your reader will know how you feel about what has happened.

Bad dreams . . .

If you find your child is having a nightmare

- Don't disturb or shake your child if he or she is still asleep. Waking a sleeping child will only frighten him or her more.
- Never get cross when your child has a nightmare. Your child is really frightened and needs comfort, not scolding.
- Assure your child that it's only a dream, that it isn't real.
- Try to get your child to talk about what happened in the dream. Talking about dreams makes them less frightening.
- Stay in the room and near the bed until your child falls asleep again.
- Turn on the lights and talk softly to soothe and reassure your child that he or she is safe.
- Use a night light or leave a landing light on. Many children are afraid of the dark.
- Let your child sleep in a room close to your bedroom.
- Watch to make sure your child doesn't do anything to hurt him- or herself, like falling out of bed.
- Nightmares sometimes lead to sleep-walking. If this occurs, guide your child gently back to bed without waking him or her.

There are things you can do which may help to prevent your child having nightmares:

- Keep the room safe in case of sleep-walking. Avoid upper bunks and keep the floor free of dangerous obstructions.
- Warn babysitters or other family members and let them know how to deal with nightmares.
- Establish a bedtime routine with a peaceful atmosphere, eg a relaxing bath, hot chocolate and a favourite story.
- Give your child a hug when you tuck him or her in.
- Check for a temperature or illness that may be causing the nightmares.
- If your child has a bad night, talk it over in the morning.
- Try to reduce stresses in the home. Children find it very distressing if their parents argue with each other.
- Ask your child if he or she is unhappy at school. Is he or she being bullied or getting into trouble?
- Prevent children watching violent or frightening television programmes or films, especially close to bedtime.

COMPREHENSION

A Write 'true' or 'false' for each of these statements.

1 If a child is having a nightmare you should wake them up.

2 Get the child to talk about what has happened in the nightmare.

3 Many children are afraid of the dark.

4 Find out if the child is having problems at school.

5 Let the child watch a horror film before going to bed.

B 1 What do you think might happen if a child is shaken and woken up in the middle of a nightmare?

2 If a child is likely to have nightmares, why do you think it is a good idea for them to sleep in a room close to his or her parents?

3 Why do you think it is important to keep the bedroom tidy if a child has nightmares?

4 What might be causing the nightmares?

5 Who do you think this advice is written for?

C 1 Do you agree that watching '*violent or frightening television programmes*' can be the cause of nightmares? Why? Why not?

2 What do you think are the most likely causes of nightmares?

VOCABULARY

Use a dictionary and the context of the advice to explain the meaning of these words. They are underlined in the passage. The first one is done for you.

1 scolding = *telling off* **2** soothe **3** occurs

4 obstructions **5** establish **6** prevent

SPELLING

Prefixes

Remember! A **prefix** is a group of letters put at the beginning of a word to change its meaning. The prefix **re** means again,
eg visit ***re****visit* (visits again)

A What do these **re** words mean? The first one is done for you.

1 reassure = *to give comfort again* **2** recount

3 recover **4** redouble

5 renew **6** repay

B Use three of the **re** words in sentences of your own.

HINT

Use a dictionary to help you.

GRAMMAR AND PUNCTUATION

Subject and predicate

Every sentence has a **subject**.
The subject is the person, place or thing the sentence is about,
eg '*Many children are afraid of the dark.*'
Many children = subject

The rest of the sentence is called the **predicate**,
eg **are afraid of the dark** = predicate

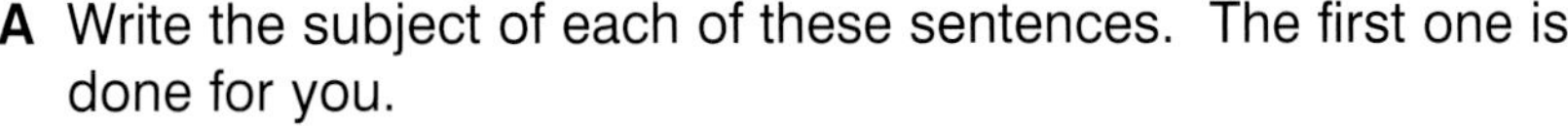

A Write the subject of each of these sentences. The first one is done for you.

1. Some children sleepwalk. *Some children*
2. Your child is really frightened.
3. A light should be left on at night.
4. Nightmares can be caused by different things.
5. An illness may be causing the nightmares.

B Copy each subject. Add an interesting predicate to each subject to complete each sentence.

1. My worst nightmare____________________________.
2. My brother ________________________________.
3. Many children _____________________________.
4. The horror film _____________________________.
5. Some people________________________________.

C Underline the verb in each of your sentences.

WRITING

Writing to advise

Advice gives you various suggestions to help you with a problem,
eg things you might do to get a Saturday job.

A set of instructions is a list of things you must do to get a result,
eg
- instructions to bake a cake
- instructions to build a model.

Language features

Sentences

Advice is easier to read if it is written in short, simple sentences. Which is easier to read?

- '*Don't disturb or shake your child if he or she is still asleep.*'
- If you find that your child is still asleep when you go into the bedroom, it is not a good idea to try to wake him or her up or disturb him or her in any way.

Order

Instructions need to be set out in the order you have to do things. Advice does not have to be in any particular order.

Imperative verbs

Using imperative verbs helps to keep the sentences short and simple,
eg '***Stay** in the room ...*' '***Turn** on the lights ...*'

Using imperative verbs means you don't have to keep repeating yourself,
eg *You should stay in the room ...*
You should turn on the lights ...

Vocabulary

Advice is usually written in a formal style,
eg '*Guide your child gently back to bed ...*' not
You should try to get the kid back in bed.

Writing assignment

Write a list of suggestions to advise someone how to go about one of these tasks:

- getting a Saturday job
- improving their fitness
- finding a new hobby.

Vesuvius explodes . . .

Pliny the Younger was born around AD 62 in the north of Italy. At the age of 17 he visited his uncle and saw the eruption of the volcano, Vesuvius. He wrote to a friend called Tacitus to tell him what had happened.

My dear Tacitus,

I was with my uncle at Miseum on the 24th August AD 79. Between two and three in the afternoon my mother pointed to an unusually big cloud which was rising from a mountain some way away. We later found out that this mountain was called Vesuvius. Some of the cloud was white but in other parts there were dark patches of dirt and ash. My uncle was <u>determined</u> to see it from closer at hand.

He ordered a boat to be made ready and was about to leave when a letter arrived from his friend, Rectina. Her villa was at the foot of Vesuvius and she was terrified of what was happening. In the letter she asked my uncle to come and rescue her. He ordered more boats to be made ready so he could rescue Rectina and as many other people as possible.

As he sailed nearer to Vesuvius, he saw many people fleeing but he kept on going. All the time he kept his eyes on the shape of the evil cloud. Ash was falling onto the boats and, as they got nearer, bits of falling rock hit them. The rocks were blackened and burned by the fire which raged in the mountain. It was impossible to get to the shore because of the ash and rocks from the volcano so he decided to make for the other side of the bay.

A wind, blowing from the sea to the shore, helped the boat to land there. My uncle immediately saw his friend, Pomponianus. He had not been able to escape in his boat because the wind was blowing in the wrong direction. He was very frightened and my uncle did his best to comfort him.

By this time it was night and everyone could see the huge flames which were lighting up Vesuvius. My uncle and Pomponianus discussed what to do. Would they be safer inside or in the open air? Many buildings were being shaken by the explosions coming from the volcano but outside was just as dangerous. It was a difficult choice but finally they decided to risk staying outside.

They tied pillows on their heads as protection against the shower of debris. By this time it should have been daylight, but the ash falling from the volcano and hanging in the air made it dark and murky. They lit torches and went down to the shore. The sea was rough and escape by boat was impossible. My uncle asked for water and rested under a sail for protection. Then came the smell of deadly sulphur, belched out from Vesuvius. My uncle stood up and immediately collapsed. He found it difficult to breathe in the dust-laden air and so he died.

Two days later, his body was found untouched, unharmed, in the clothing he had had on. He looked more asleep than dead.

Farewell.

Based on Pliny Letter 6.16

COMPREHENSION

A Copy these sentences. Fill in the missing words.

1. The mountain with the dark clouds above it was called _ _ _ _ _ _ _ _.
2. Rectina sent a letter asking Pliny's uncle to _ _ _ _ _ _ her.
3. It was impossible to get to shore because of the _ _ _ and the _ _ _ _ _.
4. Pliny's uncle landed on the other side of the _ _ _.
5. His body was found on the shore _ _ _ days later.

B **1** What was the first sign that something was wrong?

2 Explain the meaning of:
a '*closer at hand*' **b** '*at the foot of*'

3 Why do you think Pliny's uncle '*kept his eyes on the shape of the evil cloud*' as he sailed nearer?

4 Why do you think staying outside was just as dangerous as sheltering inside?

5 How do you know that Pliny's uncle had not died by being hit by falling rocks or by being burnt?

C What sort of person do you think Pliny's uncle was? Give your reasons.

VOCABULARY

Use a dictionary and the context of the letter to explain the meaning of these words. They are underlined in the passage. The first one is done for you.

1 determined = had decided	**2** fleeing	**3** raged
4 debris	**5** murky	**6** belched

SPELLING

Homophones

Homophones are words which have the same sound but different spellings and meanings

eg *to* *two* *too*
there *their* *they're*

A Find the homophones of these words in the letter. The first one is done for you.

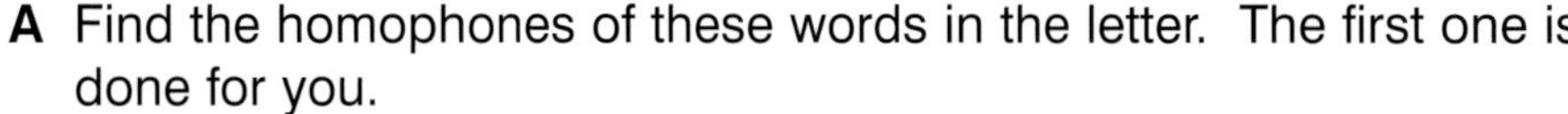

1 weigh = way	**2** sum	**3** sea
4 maid	**5** sore	**6** bean
7 knight	**8** witch	**9** buy

B Choose five of the homophones in **A** and use them in sentences of your own.

GRAMMAR AND PUNCTUATION

Compound sentences

A simple sentence is made up of one main clause and makes sense by itself,

eg *The mountain was called Vesuvius.*

A **compound sentence** is made up of two simple sentences joined by a conjunction,

eg Simple sentences:

- *The mountain was called Vesuvius.*
- *It erupted in AD 79.*

Compound sentence:

The mountain was called Vesuvius ***and*** *it erupted in AD 79.*

simple sentence — conjunction — simple sentence

A Make these simple sentences into compound sentences using the conjunctions in the box. The first one is done for you.

and but or

1 Some of the cloud was white. In other parts it was dark.
Some of the cloud was white but in other parts it was dark.

2 Rectina lived at the foot of Vesuvius. She was terrified.

3 Should he go? Should he stay?

4 Pomponianus tried to escape. The wind was blowing in the wrong direction.

5 Should they stay inside? Should they go outside?

B Copy these compound sentences. Underline the two main clauses in red and circle the conjunction. The first one is done for you.

1 Vesuvius erupted in AD 79 and hundreds of people were killed.
Vesuvius erupted in AD 79 (and) hundreds of people were killed.

2 Pliny's uncle tried to reach the shore but the rocks and ash held him back.

3 The sea was rough and escape by boat was impossible.

4 My uncle stood up and immediately collapsed.

5 He was found dead but he had not been hit by falling rocks.

WRITING

Recounting an event

Pliny's letter is an example of non-fiction writing.
What he writes about actually happened.
He **recounts** the events about the eruption of Vesuvius and how his uncle died.

Language features

Ordering paragraphs

When you recount what has happened you write the events in order. This helps the reader to understand exactly what happened.

Read each paragraph and write brief notes on the order in which Pliny recounts what happened.

Purpose and audience

You should always know why you are writing and who your audience is. Pliny is writing:

- to recount what has happened = purpose
- to his friend = audience

Pliny was always clear about why he was writing and who his audience was. He wrote:

> '*... it is one thing to write a letter, another to write history, one thing to write to a friend, another to write for the public.*'

What do you think the differences are?

Writing in the past tense

If you are recounting something that has happened you need to use the past tense,

eg '*... my mother* ***pointed*** *...*' '*... she* ***asked*** *...*' '*As he* ***sailed*** *...*'

Writing assignment

Imagine you are Pliny's uncle and that you wrote a letter about what had happened before you died. You must decide:

- why you are writing the letter
- who you are writing to.

Remember to:

- recount the events in the order that they happened to you
- write in the first person.

Fires can engulf a home in 60 seconds!
Are you prepared with a quick and safe method of escape? You would not want to be trapped in a burning building. Smoke detectors and heat alarms may warn you, but you still need a safe method of escape from a burning building.

MAKE YOUR PLANS – JUST IN CASE!

- Make sure that everyone in the family knows what to do in case of fire.
- Encourage everyone to sound a family alarm: yelling, banging on walls, blowing whistles, etc.
- Check to see if there are at least two ways to escape from every room.
- Make sure that stairs, hallways and windows can be used as fire escape routes.
- Test windows and doors – do they open easily? Are they big enough for people to escape through?
- Always sleep with the bedroom doors closed. This will keep lethal heat and smoke out of the bedrooms, giving you time to escape.
- It is a good idea to keep a torch and a whistle or bell in each bedroom.
- Practice evacuating the building blindfolded. In a real fire situation, the amount of smoke generated will make it difficult to see.
- Choose a safe meeting place outside the house.

IF A FIRE STARTS!

- In a fire, time is critical. Don't waste time getting dressed. Don't search for pets or valuables. Just get out!
- Roll out of bed. Stay low. One breath of smoke or gas may kill you!
- Feel all doors before opening. If a door is hot, escape by another route.
- Stop, drop to the ground and roll if clothes catch fire.

KEEP YOUR FAMILY SAFE

- Install smoke detectors and check once a month. Change the batteries at least once a year. There should be one smoke detector on every level of a building.
- When you are cooking, keep the handles of pans turned inwards. If oil or grease catches fire, carefully slide a lid over the pan and smother the flames. Turn off the burner.
- If an electric appliance smokes or has an unusual smell, unplug it immediately and have it repaired.
- Never tamper with the fuse box.

COMPREHENSION

A Write 'true' or 'false' for each statement.

1. You need a safe method of escape from a burning building.
2. If there is a fire, never yell or bang on the walls.
3. Make sure all the family knows where to meet outside the house.
4. At least one smoke detector should be fitted in every building.
5. If oil or grease catches fire, throw water over it.

B **1** Why do you think you need '*two ways to escape from every room*'?

2 Why should you '*Choose a safe meeting place outside the house*'?

3 Why do you think people should not get dressed and search for pets and valuables when a fire starts?

4 Why do you think you should not try to escape through a door that feels '*hot*'?

5 When cooking, why do you think you should keep '*the handles of pans turned inward*'?

C What advice would you give about matches and lighters so they do not accidentally cause a fire?

VOCABULARY

Use a dictionary and the context of the leaflet to explain the meaning of these words. They are underlined in the passage. The first one is done for you.

1 engulf = swamp	**2** lethal	**3** evacuating
4 generated	**5** appliance	**6** tamper

SPELLING

Homophones

Homophones are words which have the same sound but have different spellings and meanings.

eg *to* *two* *too*

there *their* *they're*

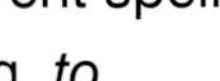

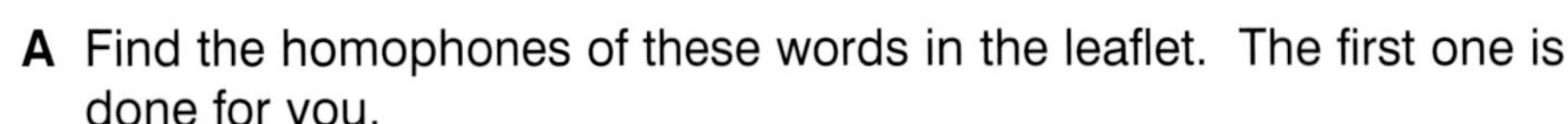

A Find the homophones of these words in the leaflet. The first one is done for you.

1 wood = would	**2** knot	**3** knead
4 waist	**5** role	**6** sea
7 stares	**8** roots	**9** threw

B Choose five of the homophones in **A** and use them in sentences of your own.

GRAMMAR AND PUNCTUATION

Sentences

Remember:

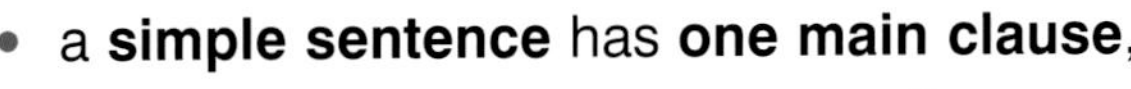

- a **simple sentence** has **one main clause**,
  eg *Smoke detectors can save lives.*

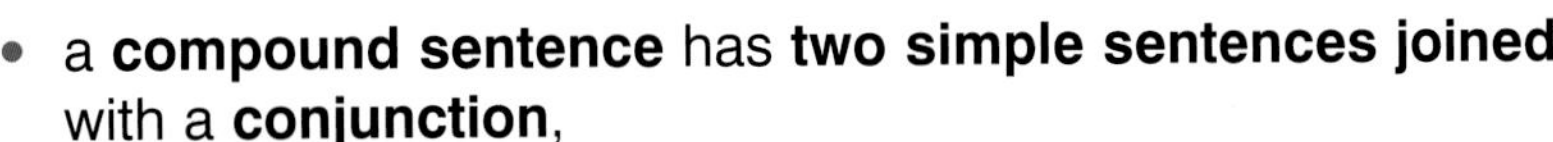

- a **compound sentence** has **two simple sentences joined** with a **conjunction**,
  eg *Smoke detectors can save lives (but) they should be checked regularly.*

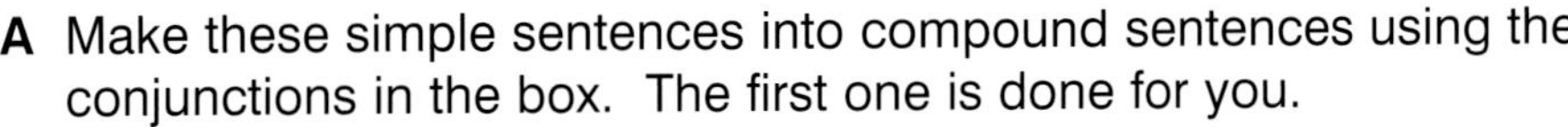

A Make these simple sentences into compound sentences using the conjunctions in the box. The first one is done for you.

and	but	or

1 The house was on fire. The fire brigade managed to save it.
The house was on fire but the fire brigade managed to save it.

2 I opened the window. I escaped.

3 Should I go down the stairs? Should I go through the window?

Complex sentences are made up of two or more clauses which are not equally important.

- You always need a main clause (simple sentence) in a complex sentence,
  eg *Smoke detectors can save lives.*
- The other clauses do not make sense on their own,
  eg *if they are checked regularly.*

(Smoke detectors can save lives) (if they are checked regularly.)
main clause second clause

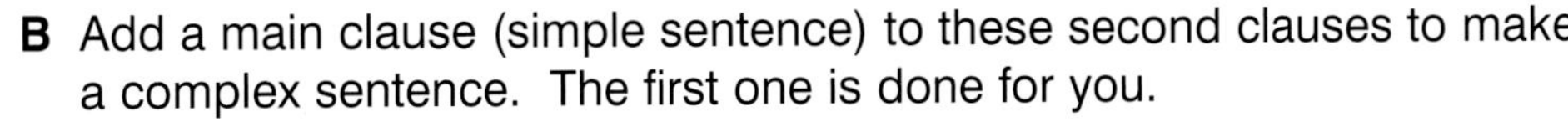

B Add a main clause (simple sentence) to these second clauses to make a complex sentence. The first one is done for you.

1 ______________________ because fire can spread quickly.
Get out of the house immediately because fire can spread quickly.

2 ______________________ even though a pet is still in the house.

3 ______________________ so you do not breathe in the smoke.

4 ______________________ while the fire brigade put out the fire.

5 ______________________ until the fire is completely out.

1.
2.
3.
4.
5.
6.

WRITING

Instructions

Part of the leaflet 'Fire Safety' is a set of **instructions**.
The instructions are in order. Things to do:

1 before a fire starts **2** when a fire has started.

Instructions should be:

- easy to follow
- in a clear order.

Language features

Purpose

The writer makes his purpose clear immediately by:

- giving the reader a shocking fact: *'Fires can engulf a home in 60 seconds!'*
- asking a question: *'Are you prepared with a quick and safe method of escape?'*

This is a set of instructions that should be taken seriously!

Audience

The writer addresses the reader directly: *'Are you ...'* *'You would not ...'*
Who are the instructions written for? Who is the *'you'*?

Organisation

The instructions are organised in a sensible way.

- *'Make your plans – Just in case!'* tells you to plan how to escape if a fire starts, eg *'Test windows and doors – do they open easily?'*
- *'If a fire starts!'* tells you what to do when a fire has started, eg *'Roll out of bed. Stay low.'*

Imperative verbs

Instructions use imperative verbs in order to:

- be as simple and as clear as possible
- avoid repetition.

You should encourage everyone ... ⟶ *'Encourage everyone ...'*
You should roll out of bed. ⟶ *'Roll out of bed.'*

Writing assignment

Write a set of instructions for one of the following:

- how to make a camp fire safely
- how to have a safe firework display.

Remember to:

- address your audience directly
- use imperative verbs
- write your instructions in a sensible order.

In the shadow of Mount Etna

What is it like to live near an active volcano? The people who live and work in the shadow of Mount Etna, Europe's biggest active volcano, can tell you.

There is a souvenir shop and other tourist kiosks very near to the crater. It was here that I met Rosa and Augusto Puleo as an explosion from the mountain rattled the windows. Their shop stands 15 feet away from an earth wall built to divert the lava flow away from the kiosks and on to waste land. An overspill of magma could, however, still bury them.

'I was never afraid of Etna,' said Rosa. 'We live with this volcano. It's like a family member and most of the time we live quite happily together.' Many of the locals, like Rosa, call the mountain "*il gigante buono*", the good giant.'

Etna has been rumbling for 12 days now and has destroyed ski-lifts and belched out huge quantities of lava. It has stopped a mere two and a half miles from the town Nicolosi.

'We are used to having lava up above,' said Alessandro Corsaro with a chuckle. 'The only difference is that now it's breathing down our necks.'

Alessandro runs a local hotel and a restaurant. Both businesses have had to be moved as both have been destroyed by lava. The mountain is rumbling again and Alessandro said, 'I hope we will be spared, but if not my brother and I, like our father and grandfather, will start again.'

Some people stroll up to the viewing points to watch the orange glow but most of the <u>inhabitants</u> of the town seem remarkably <u>disinterested</u>. The local writer Leonardo Sciascia describes Etna like this: 'It's like a huge house cat that snores quietly; every now and then it wakes, yawns, stretches lazily and with a swipe of its paw destroys a valley here or there, wiping out towns, vineyards and gardens.'

Visitors, however, take a different view. Hikers, skiers and tourists have left as the mountain rumbles on. Tourist guides in the area, that know the mountain only too well, are <u>convinced</u> that Etna will not settle down in a hurry!

Based on the *Independent on Sunday*, 29 July 2001

COMPREHENSION

A Choose the best answer.

1 The souvenir shop is:
a near the crater **b** at the edge of the crater **c** in the crater.

2 Rosa is:
a afraid of Etna **b** not afraid of Etna **c** unsure how she feels about Etna.

3 Etna has destroyed:
a the souvenir shop **b** Nicolosi **c** ski-lifts.

4 If Etna destroys Alessandro's hotel, he will:
a leave the town **b** start again **c** become a tourist guide.

5 Hikers, skiers and tourists have:
a bought souvenirs **b** bought a cat **c** left the area.

B **1** Why do you think tourists come to Mount Etna?

2 Explain these phrases:
a '*breathing down our necks*' **b** '*will be spared*'.

3 Look carefully at what Alessandro says. What sort of person do you think he is?

4 Why do you think Mount Etna is important for the people who live near it?

5 Explain in your own words why Mount Etna is described as a sleeping cat?

C How would you feel living so close to a live volcano. Why?

VOCABULARY

Use a dictionary and the context of the newspaper report to explain the meaning of these words. They are underlined in the passage. The first one is done for you.

1 crater = *mouth of a volcano* **2** divert **3** magma
4 inhabitants **5** disinterested **6** convinced

SPELLING

Soft and hard g

The letter **g** can have a **hard** sound,
eg *ma**g**ma*
The letter **g** can have a **soft** sound,
eg ***g**iant* (**g** sounds like **j**)
A **soft g** usually comes before the letters
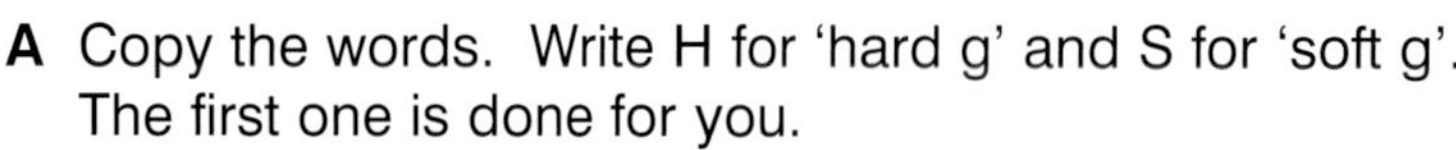
i e y

A Copy the words. Write H for 'hard g' and S for 'soft g'. The first one is done for you.

1 huge = *S* **2** again **3** grandfather
4 gentle **5** glow **6** giraffe
7 gigantic **8** gardens **9** gorgeous
10 gypsy **11** large **12** apology

HINT
Look carefully! Some words have more than one g!

B Use two **hard g** words and two **soft g** words in sentences of your own.

GRAMMAR AND PUNCTUATION

Sentences

Remember!
Complex sentences are made up of:

- a main clause = makes sense on its own
- a second clause = does not make sense on its own

Sometimes this second clause does the same job as an adverb, ie it tells us **when**, **why** and **how** the action (verb) was done.

eg *People fled in panic* *when the volcano erupted.*

main clause second clause

The second clause tells us **when** the people fled.
It begins with the conjunction **when**.

A Read each sentence carefully. Write the second (adverbial) clause in each sentence. The first one has been done for you.

1 Many tourists visited the area before Mount Etna erupted.
before Mount Etna erupted

2 Houses will be destroyed if the lava starts to flow.

3 Earth walls were built so that the town would be safe.

4 Tourists have left the area since the mountain began rumbling.

5 Tourist guides know the mountain well after working there for years.

HINT
These clauses are called adverbial.

B Copy each sentence. Finish it by choosing one of the conjunctions in the box to begin the second (adverbial) clause. The first one has been done for you.

so because even though after since

1 Mount Etna was on the news ________ it erupted so dramatically.
Mount Etna was on the news after it erupted so dramatically.

2 People have learned to live with the volcano ________ the rumblings don't worry them.

3 The tourist industry has not been very good ________ the eruptions started.

4 People live and work near Mount Etna ________ it could erupt at any time.

5 The people have returned to their homes ________ the volcano has stopped erupting.

HINT
Look for the conjunction.

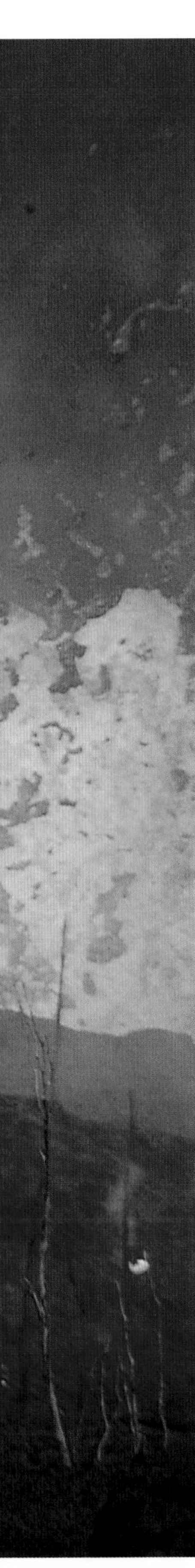

WRITING

Newspaper reports

Learning to live with Auntie Etna is a **newspaper report**.

It is news because at the time of writing Etna was rumbling. Would it erupt and cause death and destruction?

The reporter went to find out how people managed, living so close to the volcano.

Language features

Headline

It is always a good idea to have a headline which grabs the reader's attention. '*Learning to live with Auntie Etna*' gives a feeling of the mountain being threatening. Will it or won't it erupt?

Opening paragraph

Once the headline has interested the reader, the first paragraph must hold that interest. The writer here has used a question to draw you in:

'*What is it like to live near an active volcano?*'

Perhaps the reader has never thought about it **but** it might be interesting to find out!

Research

You should always know your facts before writing your report. The writer here has found out some facts,

eg '*Europe's biggest active volcano ...*' '*Etna has been rumbling for 12 days ...*'

Eye-witness accounts

Newspaper reporters often interview eye-witnesses who can tell them what they have seen, what they think and feel. Readers are more likely to believe what they are reading if what eye-witnesses say is included.

Writing assignment

Write a newspaper report on one of the following:

- Mount Etna erupts
- a local river floods the town
- a lorry spills its load in a city centre.

Remember to:

- think about the 'facts' that you are going to include in the report
- think of an eye-catching headline
- make sure your first paragraph will keep the reader interested
- use eye-witness accounts.

This is not sport…

Denys Finch Hatton went to British East Africa in 1910. He led safaris into the Serengeti so that rich visitors to the country could kill wild animals. At first these safaris were on foot. When the motor car was invented, people used it for hunting and Denys Finch Hatton did not think it was fair. Keeping up with the wild animals was much easier and many more animals were slaughtered.

He was so angry that he wrote a letter to* The Times *newspaper to persuade people that lion hunting in this area of Africa should be banned. It appeared in the paper on the 21 January 1928.

Shooting visitors to East Africa who are anxious to fill their bag as quickly as possible, are becoming increasingly numerous. Most of them want to get a lion and many of them do not care just how it is 'got'. At present there are not many easier or quicker ways of getting lion with other game thrown in than by taking a motor car to the Serengeti Plains ... I heard of one party which came away from a fortnight's trip with nearly thirty assorted lions, lionesses and cubs – an orgy of slaughter ... It is possible for sportsmen to get lions by ordinary hunting methods ... in many districts they still abound ...

The argument that the revenue would be lost for shooting licences is unsound in my opinion. I believe that many more people would be willing to pay for the privilege of seeing ... game and for photographing rather than shooting them. It will be seen from my account that the key to the situation is to be found in the motor car. It is only by proper use of the motor car ... that the great pleasure and privilege of observing these animals can at present be enjoyed. And it is by abuse of the motor car for shooting purposes, training the animals sooner or later to connect it with man ... that this privilege will be destroyed.

If anything is to be done, it must be done quickly. Is it too much to hope that ... bodies and individuals who have an interest in natural science and study and photography of wild animals in their natural surroundings ... will bestir themselves in time ... before it is too late?

Based on a letter by Denys Finch Hatton, The Times, *21 January 1928*

COMPREHENSION

A Copy these sentences. Fill in the missing words.

1. Denys Finch Hatton led _ _ _ _ _ _ _ into the Serengeti Plains.
2. He was angry when people began to hunt using _ _ _ _ _ _ _ _ _.
3. He wanted lion hunting in this part of Africa to be _ _ _ _ _ _.
4. He thought people would pay to _ _ _ _ _ _ _ _ _ _ _ the animals rather than shoot them.
5. He hoped that something would be done _ _ _ _ _ _ _.

B 1 Explain in your own words the meaning of the following:
a *'fill their bag'* **b** *'get a lion'* **c** *'an orgy of slaughter'*

2 Why do you think that Denys Finch Hatton thought that hunting in a motor car wasn't fair?

3 What are '*ordinary hunting methods*'?

4 Why do you think that photographing the animals would be more difficult if the animals connected the motor car '*with man*'?

5 What do you think he hoped the '*bodies and individuals who have an interest in natural sciences*' would do?

C Explain in your own words why Denys Finch Hatton wrote this letter.

VOCABULARY

Use a dictionary and the context of the letter to explain the meaning of these words. They are underlined in the passage. The first one is done for you.

1 numerous = very many **2** abound **3** revenue
4 unsound **5** abuse **6** bestir

SPELLING

Suffixes

If a word ends in **e** and the **suffix** begins with a **vowel**, drop the **e** before adding a suffix,

eg take: take + ing = *taking*
persuade: persuade + ed = *persuaded*

If a word ends in **e** and the **suffix** begins with a **consonant**, keep the **suffix**,

eg hope: hope + ful = *hopeful*
safe: safe + ly = *safely*

Copy and complete these words sums. The first one is done for you.

1 smile + ing = smiling **2** care + ful =
3 dare + ed = **4** use + ing =
5 time + ly = **6** hate + ed =
7 observe + ed = **8** shame + ful =
9 love + ly = **10** destroy + ed =

HINT
A suffix is a group of letters put at the end of a word.

GRAMMAR AND PUNCTUATION

Sentences

You can improve your sentences by thinking about the order of the clauses.

In this sentence the main clause comes first and **adverbial clause** comes second:

I couldn't bear to look *after the lion had been shot.*

main clause — adverbial clause

An adverbial clause can come before a main clause:

After the lion had been shot , *I couldn't bear to look.*

adverbial clause — comma — main clause

A Copy out the sentences. Underline the adverbial clause in each one. The first one is done for you.

1 Finch Hatton went on safari when he was in Africa.

2 Although he was a hunter, he didn't agree with shooting animals from a motor car.

3 No one knew much about the problem until he wrote to *The Times*.

4 I was very upset when I first read the letter.

5 If people took notice of the letter, hunting in motor cars might be stopped.

HINT

Adverbial clauses begin with conjunctions.

B Change the position of the adverbial clause so that it comes first in the sentence. The first one is done for you.

1 Hunting is a very popular sport although many people do not agree with it.

Although many people do not agree with it, hunting is a very popular sport.

2 I lived in Africa when I was younger.

3 Finch Hatton wrote to the newspaper because he wanted to save the lions.

4 People do not usually like seeing animals in zoos after they have seen them in the wild.

5 People must do something before it is too late.

HINT

Remember the comma!

WRITING

Letters to persuade

Denys Finch Hatton wrote to *The Times* to **persuade** people with power to stop lion hunting from motor cars.

Language features

Setting the scene

The letter begins by stating clearly what he is writing about:

> *'Shooting visitors to East Africa who are anxious to fill their bag as quickly as possible are becoming increasingly numerous. Most of them want to get a lion and many of them do not care just how it is 'got'.'*

The problem

He then goes on to explain the problem:

> *'At present there are not many easier or quicker ways of getting lion with other game thrown in than by taking a motor car to the Serengeti Plains ...'*

This results in '*an orgy of slaughter*'. It is clear what he is objecting to.

Opposing arguments

He has thought of one main reason why people will not agree with him:

> *'revenue would be lost for shooting licences'*

but he has the answer:

> *'I believe that many more people would be willing to pay for the privilege of seeing ... game ... and for photographing rather than shooting them.'*

Conclusion

After he has put forward his argument he states clearly what he wants done. He wants the people with power to '*bestir themselves in time ... before it is too late*'.

Writing assignment

Choose one of these topics:

- animals should not be kept in zoos
- foxes should not be hunted for sport.

Write a letter to a newspaper to persuade people to agree with you.

Remember to:

- use your first paragraph to make it clear what you are writing about
- put the arguments which will persuade people to agree with you
- mention opposing arguments and show how they are wrong
- finish by saying what you would like to be done.

The African wild dog . . .

The African wild dog can be found from the Sahara Desert down to South Africa. They roam in deserts, grasslands and even snow-covered areas.

PHYSICAL DESCRIPTION

The African wild dog is about 75 cm high at the shoulder. It is about 75–100 cm long and its tail, 30–40 cm has a white tip. It has a short, black-brown coat covered in white and yellow blotches. The dog's muzzle is short and its ears are large.

These dogs do not have very keen eyesight. They see things mainly in shades of black, white and grey and can often miss an animal if it remains still.

Their sense of smell is truly amazing. They have far more sensory cells in the nose than a human. We have about 5 million whereas they have about 140 million!

The African wild dog has very good hearing. The large ears have 17 muscles which allows the ear to swivel to pin-point any slight noise. Our ears can pick up sounds of 29,000 vibrations a second. These dogs can pick up sounds of 35,000 vibrations a second.

LIFESTYLE

The dogs live in packs of anything from 3 to 30 in number. These packs include both males and females, with one leader of each sex. Once every year, the two leaders mate but the other dogs do not. If a litter of pups is born to another female, the lead female would kill them.

HUNTING

The wild dogs are able to run for long distances which means that they can bring down swift animals such as antelope or cheetah. They work as a team as they chase their prey. When the leaders begin to tire, they drop to the back of the pack and others take over the lead. When the animal is finally brought down, the dogs use their long jaw and powerful teeth, gobbling and swallowing rather than chewing.

Based on David Taylor's Animal Assassins, *by David Taylor*

COMPREHENSION

A Write 'true' or 'false' for each of these statements.

1. Wild dogs are found only in South Africa.
2. They will live in snow-covered areas.
3. The dog's tail has a yellow tip.
4. They have a very good sense of smell.
5. They always live in packs of over 30.

B **1** How long is the African wild dog, including its tail?

2 How could an animal avoid being spotted by one of these dogs?

3 Give two reasons why the African wild dog can hear so well.

4 How many litters of pups survive in a pack each year? Why?

5 In your own words, explain how the dogs work as a team when chasing their prey.

C Using the information about the African wild dog, copy and complete the fact file.

Fact file: The African wild dog	
Height 75 cm to the shoulder	Sight
Length	Smell
Teeth	Hearing

VOCABULARY

Use a dictionary and the context of the passage to explain the meaning of these words. They are underlined in the passage. The first one is done for you.

1 muzzle = animal's face **2** keen **3** sensory cells

4 swivel **5** litter **6** prey

SPELLING

Plurals

These are the rules for making words ending in **o** plural.

1 Usually we add **es**, eg *dingo* *dingo**es***

2 We just add **s** for:

- words ending in **oo**, eg *cuckoo* *cuckoo**s***
- musical words, eg *cello* *cello**s***
- abbreviations (shortened words), eg *hippo* *hippo**s***

Write the plural answer for each clue. The first one is done for you.

1 red salad fruit — begins with t — tomatoes

2 musical instrument with black and white notes — begins with p

3 taken with a camera (abbreviation) — begins with p

4 vegetable for making chips — begins with p

5 painting on the skin — begins with t

GRAMMAR AND PUNCTUATION

Active and passive verbs

In a sentence:

- the subject does the action
- the verb is the action
- the object has the action done to it,

eg (*Wild dogs*) (*killed*) (*the antelope.*)
subject — verb — object

This pattern: subject + verb + object = **active voice**

A Copy these active sentences. Underline the subject in red, the verb in blue and the object in green. The first one is done for you.

1. The dog bared its teeth.
2. The pack hunted the cheetah.
3. The hunting dogs smelled the scent.
4. The dogs could not see the motionless animal.
5. The female leader ate the pups.

Some sentences have a different pattern.

The (antelope) was (killed) by the (wild dogs.)
object — verb — subject

This pattern: object + verb + subject = **passive voice**

B Copy these passive sentences. Underline the object in green, the verb in blue and the subject in red. The first one is done for you.

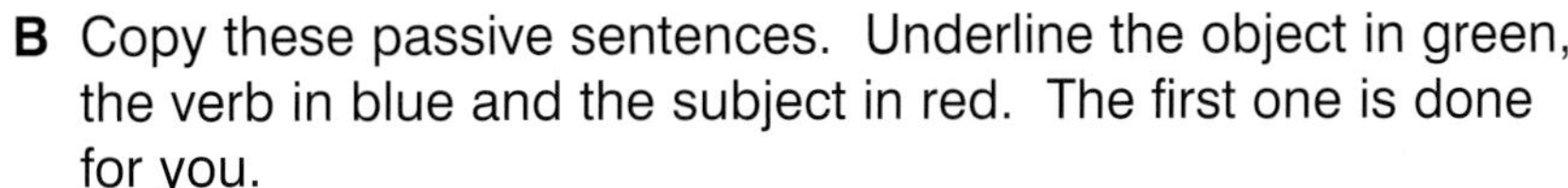

1. The teeth were bared by the dog.
2. The cheetah was hunted by the pack.
3. The scent was smelled by the hunting dogs.
4. The motionless animal was not seen by the dogs.
5. The pups were eaten by the female leader.

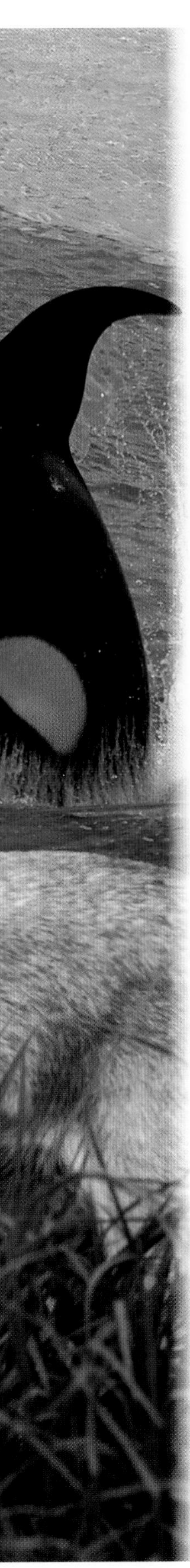

WRITING

Presenting information

There are many different ways of presenting **information**, eg

- text
- charts
- drawings
- photographs
- maps
- graphs, etc.

The writer of *The African wild dog* has presented the information in text, photographs and a map.

Language features

Research

To present information you must first research the subject. Use books, magazines, the Internet, etc to find out as much as you can. Make notes about the important information you discover.

Organising the information

Organise your information so that the reader finds it easy to follow. The writer of *The African wild dog* has organised his information into paragraphs.

Paragraph	Information
1	Location
2	Physical description
3	Packs
4	Hunting

You can use sub-headings for each paragraph.

Present tense

Unless an information passage is about something that has happened in the past, it should be written in the present tense,

eg '*They* ***roam*** *...*' '*The dog's muzzle* ***is*** *...*' '*The dogs* ***live*** *...*'

Writing assignment

Choose one of the following animals to research:

- dingo
- cheetah
- killer whale.

Remember to:

- make notes from books, magazines, the Internet, etc
- order your notes into paragraphs
- use the present tense.

A cruel custom . . .

Bulgaria is one of the few places left where bears are held in captivity and made to dance in towns and villages so that their cruel owners can make money.

About 25 of these bears are dragged around the country. They have been captured from the wild or sold by disreputable zoos. What happens to them is really horrific! A thick iron ring is put through the bear's nose. This is attached to a chain which the owner yanks to make the bear dance. The ring and the chain cause such agony that the bear twitches and writhes in pain – the audience laughs and applauds the bear's 'dance'!

It is no better for the bears when they are not 'performing'! They are left chained up with little food and water. They are given no shelter from the elements and are often injured by the ring cutting into the flesh of their nose.

Dancing bears

IT HAS GOT TO STOP!

At last things are being done to stop this cruel custom. The government has now made it illegal to use bears in this way. New laws will soon be passed so that the police can arrest and fine people who try to make money out of these poor creatures.

There is a possibility that a bear sanctuary will be opened where rescued bears can live in peace, free from the pain and cruelty of performing for unthinking audiences.

Generally, the Bulgarian people are not interested in dancing bears; it is tourists who give money to see them which keeps this barbaric tradition on its last legs. Posters are being put up in bars and hotels to plead with tourists not to give money to these wicked people.

What can you do?

- Don't pay money to watch the bears.
- Complain to your tour operator if you see dancing bears.
- Write to the Bulgarian Embassy.

BACK

Based on 'Bulgaria's dancing bears', WSPA, 4 October 2001

COMPREHENSION

A Choose the best answer for each question.

1 People keep dancing bears:
a as pets **b** for protection **c** to make money.

2 In Bulgaria, there are:
a about 25 bears **b** less than 25 bears **c** more than 25 bears.

3 Laws will soon be passed so that the police:
a can own dancing bears **b** can arrest the owners **c** can watch dancing bears.

4 Posters are put up to:
a advertise dancing bears **b** educate tourists **c** sell dancing bears.

5 If you see one you should:
a complain **b** pay to watch **c** set it free.

B **1** Explain the meaning of these phrases:
a *'held in captivity'* **b** *'There is a possibility'* **c** *'on its last legs'*

2 How is the writer trying to make you feel by using such words as *'horrific'*, *'cruel'* and *'barbaric'*?

3 How are the bears treated when:
a they are performing **b** they are not performing?

4 Why does the writer describe the audience as *'unthinking'*?

5 If you wrote to the Bulgarian Embassy, what do you think the writer wants you to say?

C What do you think is the writer's purpose in putting this article on the website?

VOCABULARY

Use a dictionary and the context of the web article to explain the meaning of these words. They are underlined in the passage. The first one is done for you.

1 disreputable = *bad reputation* **2** horrific **3** writhes
4 elements **5** sanctuary **6** plead

SPELLING

Silent letters

Some words have silent letters which we do not sound,
eg **k**now **w**rite tom**b**

A The answers to these clues have a silent (K)

1 You can tie this with string. **2** a joint in the leg
3 You do this with wool and needles. **4** used for cutting

B The answers to these clues have a silent (W)

1 You fence with this. **2** A question needs one.
3 the joint between your hand and arm **4** You do this to a present.

C The answers to these clues have a silent (B)

1 a baby sheep **2** You use this to tidy your hair.
3 You have one on each hand. **4** a burial chamber

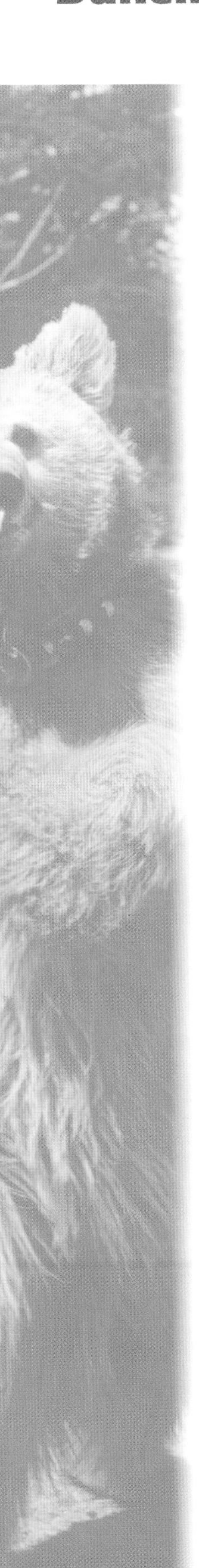

GRAMMAR AND PUNCTUATION

Semi-colons

This is a **semi-colon** ;

It is used to separate items in a **list** of statements in a sentence,

eg *The bear was on its last legs; the chain was causing it pain; its nose was bleeding; and it was badly injured.*

The statements about:

- the chain
- the bleeding nose
- the injuries

explain why: *The bear was on its last legs.*

A Copy out the sentences and add the semi-colons. The first one is done for you.

1 The owners are very cruel they make money out of the bears they treat them horribly and they do not give them enough food and water.

The owners are very cruel; they make money out of the bears; they treat them horribly; and they do not give them enough food and water.

2 When I was in Bulgaria I saw lots of interesting things beautiful villages magnificent mountains and fascinating buildings.

3 In the town that day there were many tourists locals doing their shopping school children on a trip and a colourful parade.

A **semi-colon** is also used to separate **two statements** in a sentence.

These statements balance each other,

eg [1] *Generally, the Bulgarian people are not interested in dancing bears*; [2] *it is the tourists who give money to see them which keeps this barbaric custom on its last legs.*

Statement 1: those who do not support dancing bears

Statement 2: those who do support dancing bears.

B Copy out the sentences and add the semi-colons. The first one is done for you.

1 Dancing bears have been stopped in Greece they can still be seen in Bulgaria.

Dancing bears have been stopped in Greece**;** they can still be seen in Bulgaria.

2 Tourists watch the dancing bears local people are not interested.

3 If you give money to the owners you are supporting them if you do not give money dancing bears will stop.

WRITING

Inform and persuade

The purpose of the web article *Dancing bears* is:

- to **inform** readers about how these animals are suffering
- to **persuade** readers that it must be stopped.

Language features

Information

The writer has researched the subject to give us the facts:

- He uses statistics, eg '*About 25 of these bears...*'
- He has found out where the bears come from, eg '*captured from the wild or sold by disreputable zoos*'.
- He knows how they are treated, eg '*dragged around*', '*given no shelter*'.
- He is aware of the current law, eg '*The government has now made it illegal*'.

Persuasive language

The writer has used two ways to persuade us to agree with his point of view:

- Language that makes us feel pity for the bears, eg

'horrific' *'cruel'* *'barbaric'* *'writhes'* *'injured'*

- A direct appeal to us, the readers, to help stop the situation, eg

'Don't *pay money ...'* ***'Complain*** *...'* ***'Write*** *...'*

He uses imperative verbs to 'order' us to do something!

Writing assignment

Choose something you think is unjust or cruel, eg

- fox hunting
- caged birds
- fishing.

Write an article to go on the Internet to persuade people that you are right.

Plan your article.

1. Explain what cruel thing you are writing about.
2. Explain what goes on.
3. Explain if anything has been done to stop it.
4. Tell readers what they can do to help.

Remember to:

- find out the facts
- use persuasive language.

BRITAIN · NEEDS
YOU · AT · ONCE
PUBLISHED BY THE PARLIAMENTARY RECRUITING COMMITTEE. LONDON. POSTER Nº 108.
PRINTED BY SPOTTISWOODE & Cº LTD LONDON, E.C.

The First World War …

When Britain was at war in 1914–1918 people were needed for combat.

- *The regular army*: These were people who had already joined the army as a job before war broke out.
- *Volunteers*: With the advent of war, many young men volunteered. They were eager to join up to be part of what they saw as a 'great adventure'.
- *Conscription*: As the war dragged on and many thousands of soldiers had been killed, it was more difficult to find volunteers. People were then 'conscripted'. This meant they were ordered to go and fight and they could be imprisoned for refusing.

It was considered that volunteers made better soldiers than those who had been conscripted. The government tried to persuade people that it was an heroic thing to fight for their country. Posters were stuck on billboards and advertisements were put in newspapers. This campaign was to persuade people that the enemy was evil and that right was on our side. This kind of advertising is called propaganda.

COMPREHENSION

A Copy these sentences. Fill in the missing words.

1. The First World War lasted from 1914 to _ _ _ _.
2. Volunteers were _ _ _ _ _ to join up.
3. People who were ordered to join up were _ _ _ _ _ _ _ _ _ _ _.
4. People could be _ _ _ _ _ _ _ _ _ _ if they refused to join up.
5. The government used a campaign of _ _ _ _ _ _ _ _ _ _ to persuade people to fight.

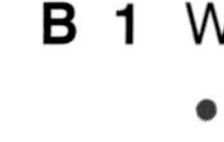

B **1** Who or what do you think is represented by:
- the knight on the horse
- the dragon?

2 Why do you think the poster is so colourful?

3 Why do you think there is not much writing on the poster?

4 What is the purpose of the poster?

5 Who do you think the poster is aimed at?

C Write a few sentences to explain how you might have felt seeing this poster if:
- you were a young man eager to join up
- you were a woman whose husband had died in battle.

VOCABULARY

Use a dictionary and the context of the passage to explain the meanings of these words. They are underlined in the passage. The first one is done for you.

1 combat = fighting **2** advent **3** eager

4 imprisoned **5** heroic **6** campaign

SPELLING

Spelling by analogy

Analogy means similarity. If you can spell one word you can probably spell other words in the family,

eg If you can spell ***adventure***,
you can spell *adventurous* *misadventure*.

If you can spell ***eager***,
you can spell ***eagerly*** ***eagerness***.

A Put these words into their family groups. There are four family groups for you to find. Each family group has three words.

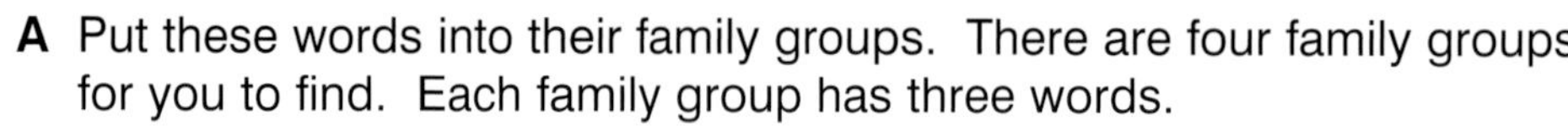

refuse	kind	imprison	volunteer	refusing	voluntary
refused	kindly	prison	unkind	prisoner	volunteering

B For each word, write two more family words.

1 join **2** persuade

3 great **4** drag

5 young **6** advertise

GRAMMAR AND PUNCTUATION

Direct and reported speech

Direct speech is when we use speech marks at the beginning and end of the words *actually spoken*,

eg *'You should join up today!' barked the officer.*

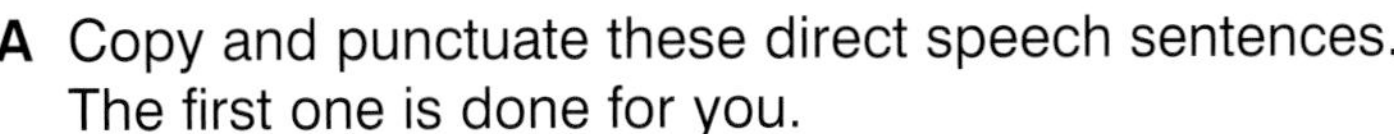

opening speech marks spoken words closing speech marks

A Copy and punctuate these direct speech sentences. The first one is done for you.

1 Are you going to join the army asked his father.

'Are you going to join the army?' asked his father.

2 Volunteers make better soldiers than conscripts said the general.

3 We need more soldiers said the officer.

4 War is a dreadful thing said the old man.

HINT

Remember the punctuation goes before the closing speech marks.

When we write about what a person said but do not use their actual words, this is **reported speech** and we do not need the speech marks,

eg *The officer said that they should join up today.*

B Write each of these sentences in reported speech. The first one is done for you.

1 'The war has lasted longer than we expected,' said the general.

The general said that the war had lasted longer than they expected.

2 'Our men are very tired,' complained the sergeant.

3 'When are the new soldiers arriving?' asked the officer.

4 'They should be here next week,' replied the general.

C Write each of these sentences in direct speech. The first one is done for you.

1 Sam said that he wanted to join the army.

'I want to join the army,' said Sam.

2 His mother asked him why he wanted to do such a stupid thing.

3 His father told him he was not old enough to join up.

4 Sam said that it wasn't fair.

ARMY
BE THE BEST
OPPORTUN
EAVERS
PLEASE GIVE BL♥♥D

WRITING

Using pictures to persuade

The propaganda posters have very few words. They get the message across by the use of **pictures**. The pictures stick in the mind and people do not have to stop for a long time to read lots of words.

Language features

Short and to the point

There are very few words on the poster,

eg BRITAIN NEEDS YOU AT ONCE

They are:

- written in capitals so they stand out
- short and to the point
- very clear so everyone gets the message.

Pictures

Pictures have to mean something. The pictures on the poster are of St George and the dragon. Everyone has heard the story so they would know that:

- the knight is heroic and 'good'
- the dragon is the enemy and 'evil'.

The knight has stuck his spear into the evil dragon. The message is clear:

If you help, we will defeat the enemy!

Writing assignment

Choose one of these topics:

- joining the army
- giving blood
- giving to a charity.

Design a poster to persuade people. Think about:

- a modern hero or heroine you could use
- the words on the poster – short and to the point.

Draw your poster in rough first and plan:

- the place for the picture
- the size and style of lettering
- the colours.

Going solo ...

In his autobiography* Going Solo, *Roald Dahl tells of his experiences in the RAF. This extract is about training to be a pilot.

At the aerodrome we had three instructors and three planes. The instructors were civil airline pilots borrowed by the RAF from a small domestic company called Wilson Airways. The planes were Tiger Moths. The Tiger Moth is or was a thing of great beauty. Everyone who has ever flown a Tiger Moth has fallen in love with it. It is a totally efficient and very acrobatic little biplane powered by a Gypsy engine, and as my instructor told me, a Gypsy engine has never been known to fail in mid air. You could throw a Tiger Moth about all over the air and nothing ever broke. You could glide it upside down hanging in your straps for minutes on end, and although the engine cut out when you did that because the carburettor was also upside down, the motor started again at once when you turned her the right way up again. You could spin her vertically downwards for thousands of feet and then all she needed was a touch on the rudder-bar, a bit of throttle and the stick pushed forward and out she came in a couple of flips...

When flying a military aeroplane, you sit on your parachute, which adds another six inches to your height. When I got into the open cockpit of a Tiger Moth for the first time and sat down on my parachute, my entire head stuck up in the open air. The engine was running and I was getting a rush of wind full in the face from the slipstream.

'You are too tall,' the instructor whose name was Flying Officer Parkinson said, 'Are you sure you want to do this?'

'Yes please,' I said.

From Going Solo *by Roald Dahl*

Roald Dahl includes a letter he wrote to his mother at about the time he was learning to fly.

Nairobi
4 December 1939

Dear Mama,
I'm having a lovely time, have never enjoyed myself so much. I've been sworn into the RAF proper and am definitely in it now until the end of the war. My rank – a Leading Aircraftman, with every opportunity of becoming a pilot officer in a few months if I don't make a B.F. of myself. No boys to do everything for me anymore. Get your own food, wash your own knives and forks, fold up your own clothes, and in short, do everything for yourself. I suppose I'd better not say too much about what we do or where we are going, because the letter would probably be torn up by the censor, but we wake at 5.30 a.m., drill before breakfast till 7 a.m., fly and attend lectures till 12.30, 12.30 / 1. 30 lunch – 1.30 to 6 p.m. flying and lectures. The flying is grand and our instructors are extremely pleasant and proficient. With any luck I'll be flying solo by the end of the week...

COMPREHENSION

A Write 'true' or 'false' for each of these statements.

1. Roald Dahl learned to fly in a Tiger Moth.
2. The Tiger Moth was not a reliable aeroplane.
3. He had to fly with his parachute strapped to his back.
4. While he was training to be a pilot, he did not have to do everything for himself.
5. He spent 10 hours a day flying and attending lectures.

B **1** Why does Roald Dahl say that the Tiger Moth '*is or was*' very beautiful?

2 What do you think a '*biplane*' is?

3 Why did the engine cut out when the plane was upside down?

4 How do you know that other people used to do everything for Roald Dahl?

5 If he wrote too many details about '*what we do or where we are going*' why would the censor tear up the letter?

C In your own words, explain how you think Roald Dahl felt about flying. Explain your reasons.

VOCABULARY

Use a dictionary and the context of the passage to explain the meaning of these words. They are underlined in the passage. The first one is done for you.

1 aerodrome = *small airfield*
2 efficient
3 carburettor
4 vertically
5 slipstream
6 proficient

SPELLING

Syllables

Syllables are the sound parts of each word,

eg <u>three</u> = 1 syllable
<u>beaut / y</u> = 2 syllables
<u>com / pan / y</u> = 3 syllables

Each syllable has a **vowel** or the letter **y**.

Copy each of these words. Split them into syllables. Write the number of syllables. The first one is done for you.

1 domestic = *dom / es / tic 3 syllables*
2 fallen
3 totally
4 instructor
5 about
6 straps
7 military
8 parachute
9 entire

HINT
Splitting words into syllables helps with spelling.

GRAMMAR AND PUNCTUATION

Past tense

To make the simple **past tense** of most verbs we add **ed**,

eg power *power**ed***
start *start**ed***

If the root word ends in **e**, we drop the **e** and add **ed**,

eg lov~~e~~ + ed = *lov**ed***
settl~~e~~ + ed = *settl**ed***

A Write the past tense of these verbs. The first one is done for you.

1 smile = smiled **2** borrow **3** need
4 wave **5** play **6** hate
7 climb **8** push **9** save

Many verbs do not follow these rules. They have an **irregular past tense**,

eg have: past tense = *had*
fly: past tense = *flew*

B Write the irregular past tense of these verbs.
The first one is done for you.

1 tell past tense = told **2** spin
3 fall **4** throw
5 write **6** drink
7 think **8** fight
9 begin **10** build
11 make **12** get

HINT
Think of a verb in a 'yesterday' sentence, eg I told them yesterday.

C Use five of the past tense verbs you have made in sentences of your own.

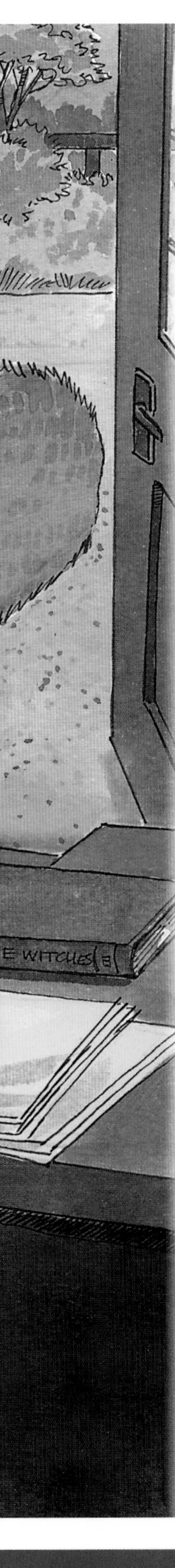

WRITING

Autobiography

An **autobiography** is when a person writes about his or her own life. In *Going Solo*, Roald Dahl writes about the experiences he had in Africa during the Second World War.

Language features

Writing in the first person

Autobiographies are written in the first person. Using 'I' or 'we' to begin every sentence can be boring. Roald Dahl has avoided doing this by:

- thinking about word order

  Instead of writing: We had three instructors and three planes at the aerodrome; he writes: '*At the aerodrome we had three instructors and three planes.*'
- using conjunctions

  Instead of writing: The engine was running. I was getting a rush of wind ... he writes: '*The engine was running and I was getting a rush of wind ...*'

Facts and events

Roald Dahl describes:

- the type of aircraft he was learning to fly in so readers can 'see' it in their imaginations
- what happened when he first got into the cockpit so readers can 'feel' the experience.

Feelings

In an autobiography we do not only want to know what happens. We want to know how the writer feels. We get to know most about his feelings in the letter to his mother, eg

'*I'm having a lovely time, have never enjoyed myself so much.*'

Writing assignment

Choose something that has happened to you and write a short autobiography to describe:

- what happened
- how you felt about it.

Remember to:

- write in the first person
- don't begin every sentence with 'I' or 'we'
- describe what happens
- describe how you felt.

Have the aliens landed . . .?

On 30 October 1938 there was an exciting broadcast on the radio. The War of the Worlds, *a novel by H G Wells, had been turned into a radio play. The story was about Martians landing on Earth and taking over the planet!*

The next day, in the *New York Times*, this headline appeared:

RADIO LISTENERS PANIC, TAKING WAR DRAMA AS FACT

It seemed that many listeners had thought that the Martians had really landed on Earth!

The *New York Times* went on to explain what it thought had happened:

> The radio listeners, apparently, missed or did not listen to the introduction which was 'The Columbia Broadcasting System ... present Orson Wells and the Mercury Theatre ... in The War of the Worlds by H G Wells'. They also failed to associate the program with the newspaper listing of the program. They ignored three announcements made during the broadcast emphasizing its fictional nature.

So, what had happened? At least 6 million people had heard the broadcast and many thousands, convinced that the Martians had landed, panicked. The *New York Times* reported on what some people had done.

> In Newark, in a single block, more than twenty families rushed out of their houses with wet handkerchiefs and towels over their heads to protect them from what they believed was to be a gas raid.

> Throughout New York families left their homes, some to flee to nearby parks.

> Thousands of persons called the police, newspapers and radio stations, seeking advice on protective measures against the raids.

> One man from Dayton, Ohio, asked, 'What time will it be the end of the world?'

People thought that enemy planes were bombing the city and local hospitals treated people for shock and hysteria. Someone rushed into a church and said that a meteor had fallen, while another man was sure he could smell the gas. He claimed: I looked out of my window and saw a greenish eerie light which I was sure came from a monster: it proved to be the lights of a car!

Based on From Other Worlds *by Hilary Evans*

COMPREHENSION

A Choose the best answer.

1 The *War of the Worlds* is about:
a radios **b** Martians **c** bombs.

2 The broadcasting company:
a explained that it was a play **b** did not explain that it was a play
c said the Martians had landed.

3 People panicked because:
a they thought the broadcast was a news report
b they did not like the play **c** they had nothing better to do.

4 People rang radio stations to:
a ask for the play to be repeated **b** ask where the nearest park was
c seek advice.

5 One man said that he thought the greenish eerie light was:
a a car **b** a monster **c** someone with a towel over their head.

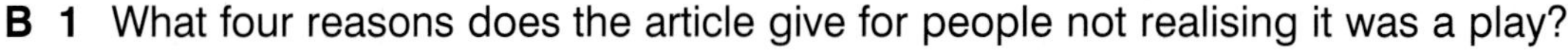

B **1** What four reasons does the article give for people not realising it was a play?

2 Why did people try to protect themselves with '*handkerchiefs and towels*'?

3 Why do you think some people fled to '*nearby parks*'?

4 One person announced that something had happened that was nothing to do with the broadcast. What was it?

5 Why do you think the panic spread to people who had not heard the broadcast?

C Look carefully at the headline from the *New York Times*:

1 Would this headline have made you want to read the article or not? Why?

2 What effect was the headline writer trying to create?

VOCABULARY

Use a dictionary and the context of the article to explain the meaning of these words. They are underlined in the passage. The first one is done for you.

1 apparently = seemingly   **2** associate   **3** fictional
4 protective   **5** hysteria   **6** eerie

SPELLING

Spelling by analogy

> Remember that **analogy** means similarity.
> If you can spell one word, you can probably spell other words in the family,
> eg If you can spell ***listen***
> you can spell *listeners* *listening*
> If you can spell ***announce***
> you can spell *announcing* *announcements*

A Put these words into their family groups. There are four family groups to find. Each family group has three words.

> appear measure thought convincing unconvinced thoughtful disappear measurement measuring thoughtless conviction appearance

B For each word, write two more family words.

1 miss   **2** exciting   **3** introduce
4 nature   **5** believe   **6** fall

GRAMMAR AND PUNCTUATION

The colon

This is a **colon** :

It is used to introduce a quotation,

eg 'The *New York Times* reported: *Throughout New York families left their homes, some to flee to nearby parks.*'

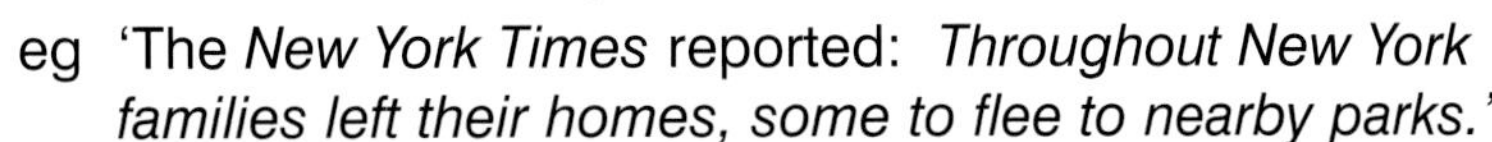

A Copy out these sentences. Add the missing colons. The first one is done for you.

1 One panic-stricken listener said 'I knew this would happen some day.'

One panic-stricken listener said: 'I knew this would happen some day.'

2 The *New York Times* reported in Newark, people believed there was going to be a gas attack.

3 One man was hysterical 'They're bombing New York!'

A **colon** can also be used to begin a list in a sentence,

eg *The following people claimed to have seen the Martians: Mr Smith, Gloria Swan and her three children.*

B Copy out these sentences. Add the missing colons. The first one is done for you.

1 There were three main reasons why people thought the Martians had landed they had missed the introduction, they had not read about the programme in the paper and they had ignored the announcements during the programme.

There were three main reasons why people thought the Martians had landed: they had missed the introduction, they had not read about the programme in the paper and they had ignored the announcements during the programme.

2 People treated at the hospital had a variety of symptoms hysteria, shock and depression.

3 What was going on Martians, bombs, meteorites?

C Write a sentence of your own using a colon.

WRITING

Newspaper reports

The *New York Times* reported what had happened on that strange evening on 30 October 1938. **Newspaper reports** are usually written very soon after an event has taken place.

Language features

Headline

This is very important. A headline has to grab the readers' attention and make them want to go on and read the whole report,

eg **RADIO LISTENERS PANIC, TAKING WAR DRAMA AS FACT**

If the headline had been: **RADIO LISTENERS MAKE A MISTAKE** do you think it would have attracted many readers?

Alliteration can be used to make attention-grabbing headlines,

eg **THOUSANDS THINK THEY ARE THREATENED FROM THE SKY.**

Make up a headline of your own for the Martian story using alliteration.

Background information

One of the questions a newspaper report has to answer is 'Why'? The report tells readers why people did not realise they were listening to a play, eg:

'They ignored three announcements made during the broadcast ...'

Factual information

Another question a newspaper report has to answer is 'What'? It has to tell readers the facts, eg:

- *'In Newark, in a single block, more than twenty families rushed out ...'*
- *'One man from from Dayton, Ohio ...'*

Eye-witness accounts

Reporters try to interview people who have been involved, eg:

- *'I looked out of my window and saw a greenish eerie light ...'*

Writing assignment

Just imagine the Martians really did land on Earth! You are a newspaper reporter and you write about the first spacecraft landing and the Martians coming out.

Remember to write:

- an attention-grabbing headline
- a description of the spacecraft
- eye-witness accounts.
- the facts – what happened
- a description of the Martians

A night at the theatre...

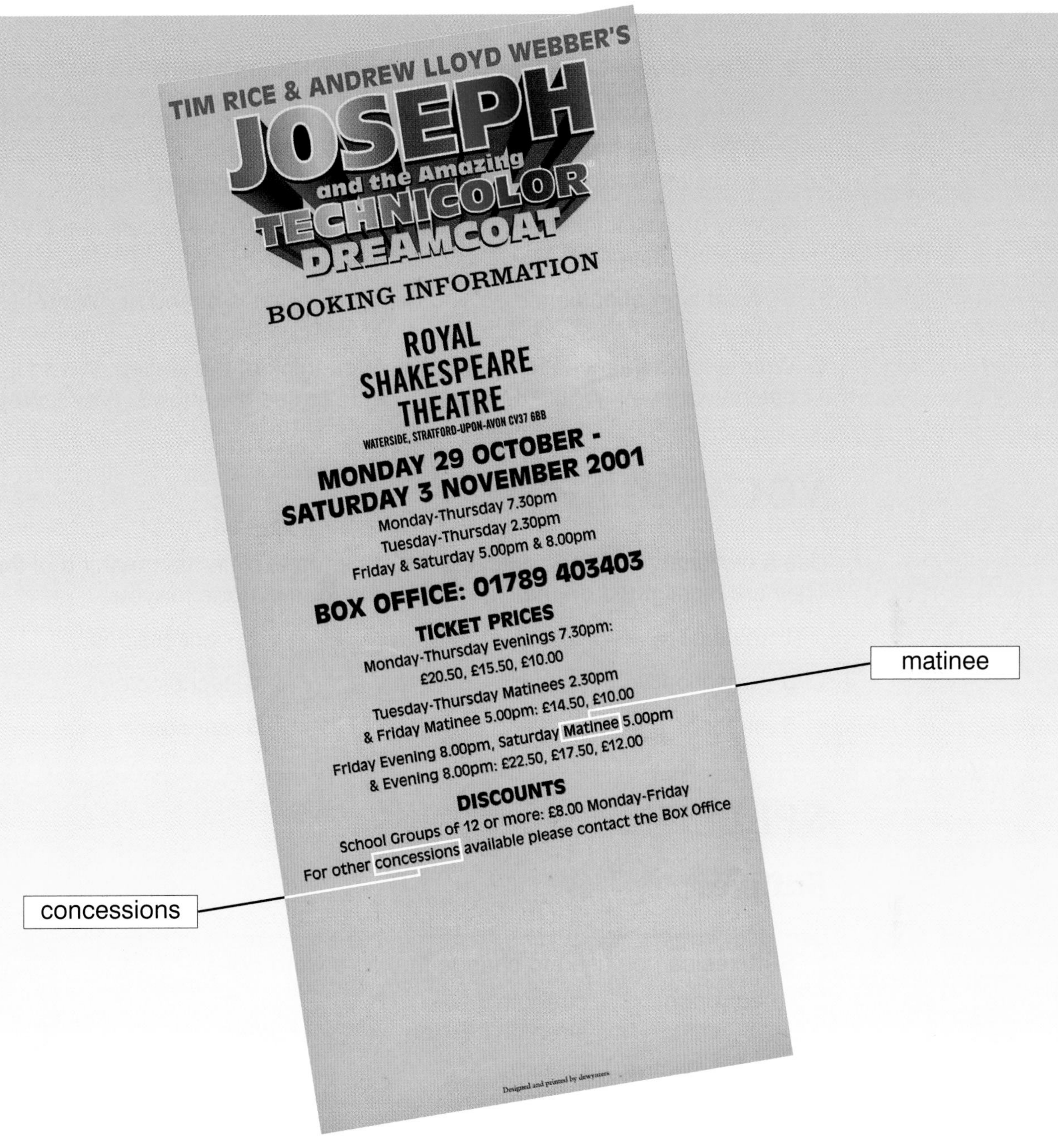

COMPREHENSION

A Copy these sentences. Fill in the missing words.

1. The musical is called 'Joseph and the _ _ _ _ _ _ _ Technicolor Dreamcoat'.
2. It is on from Monday 29 October to Saturday 3 _ _ _ _ _ _ _ _.
3. It is written by Tim _ _ _ _ and Andrew Lloyd Webber.
4. The most expensive ticket is £ _ _. _ _.
5. 01789 403403 is the telephone number of the _ _ _ _ _ _ _ _ _ _.

B **1** Where is the show being performed?

2 What do you think '*The Show of the Millennium*' means?

3 How much would it cost if two adults went to see the show on a Friday evening and bought:

- the most expensive tickets
- the cheapest tickets?

4 Why do you think the leaflet uses quotes from newspapers like the *Evening Telegraph*?

5 What type of audience do you think the leaflet is aimed at. Why?

C Write a few sentences to explain what you think of the leaflet. Would it catch your eye? Would it make you want to see the show? Why? Why not?

VOCABULARY

Use a dictionary and the context of the leaflet to explain the meaning of these words. They are highlighted on the leaflet. The first one is done for you.

1 matinee = afternoon performance

2 concessions

3 sensation

4 technicolor

5 sheer

6 encores

SPELLING

Suffixes

Suffixes can be used to change the job a word does,

eg	noun:	strength				
	verb:	strength	+	**en**	=	*strengthen*
	adjective:	modern				
	verb:	modern	+	**ise**	=	*modernise*

A Add one of these suffixes to the words below.

en ise ly

Write what job the new words does. The first one is done for you.

1 friend (noun) + ly = friendly (adjective)

2 soft (adjective)

3 magnet (noun)

4 weak (adjective)

5 general (adjective)

6 cost (noun)

B Use three of the new words you have made in sentences of your own.

GRAMMAR AND PUNCTUATION

Parts of speech

Remember, the four main **parts of speech** are:

- nouns — naming words
- adjectives — words which describe nouns
- verbs — action words or 'being' words
- adverbs — words which tell us more about verbs (how, when, where)

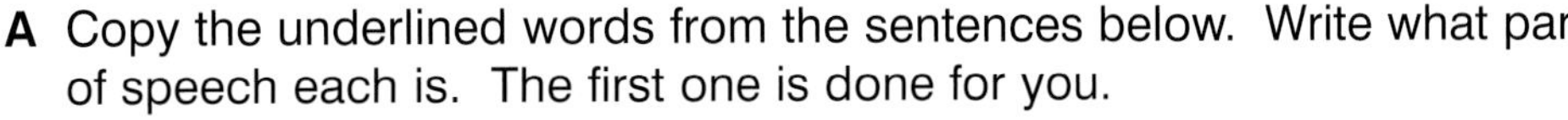

A Copy the underlined words from the sentences below. Write what part of speech each is. The first one is done for you.

1 The play was made into a film. *was made = verb*

2 The costumes for the play were very expensive.

3 The actor's make up took a long time to put on.

4 The director finally lost his temper.

5 There was loud applause when the play finished.

Some words can do more than one job,

eg
- He had to pay a **fine** because he parked in front of the theatre. fine = noun
- He was **fined** £20.00. to fine = verb
- He missed a **fine** show. fine = adjective

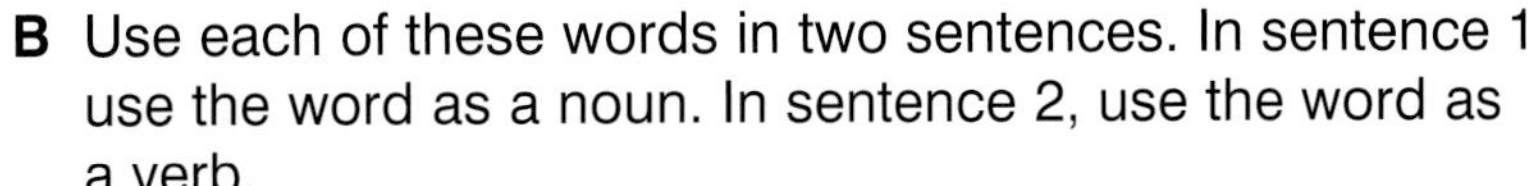

B Use each of these words in two sentences. In sentence 1, use the word as a noun. In sentence 2, use the word as a verb.

1 show 2 puzzle 3 dance

4 play 5 work 6 cast

HINT

You can put endings like 'ed' and 'ing' on the word when you use it as a verb.

C Copy and complete the table below. The first one is done for you.

Noun	Adjective	Verb	Adverb
fear	fearful	to fear	fearfully
hope			
fool			
sleep			

TIM RICE & ANDREW LLOYD WEBBER'S

JOSEPH and the Amazing TECHNICOLOR® DREAMCOAT

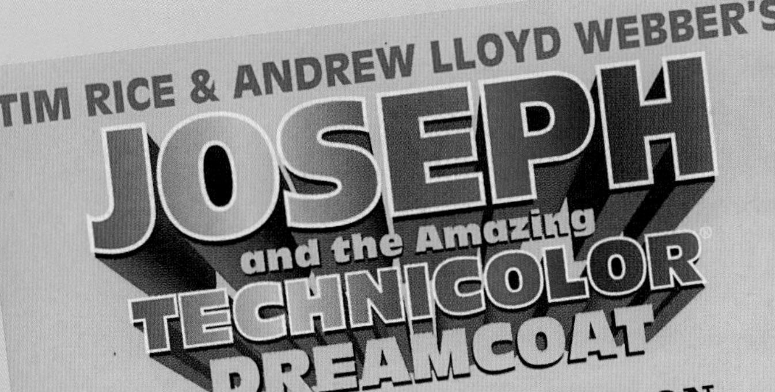

BOOKING INFORMATION

ROYAL SHAKESPEARE THEATRE

WATERSIDE, STRATFORD-UPON-AVON CV37 6BB

MONDAY 29 OCTOBER - SATURDAY 3 NOVEMBER 2001

Monday-Thursday 7.30pm
Tuesday-Thursday 2.30pm
Friday & Saturday 5.00pm & 8.00pm

BOX OFFICE: 01789 403403

TICKET PRICES

Monday-Thursday Evenings 7.30pm:
£20.50, £15.50, £10.00

Tuesday-Thursday Matinees 2.30pm
& Friday Matinee 5.00pm: £14.50, £10.00

Friday Evening 8.00pm, Saturday Matinee 5.00pm
& Evening 8.00pm: £22.50, £17.50, £12.00

DISCOUNTS

School Groups of 12 or more: £8.00 Monday-Friday
For other concessions available please contact the Box Office

Designed and printed by dewynters

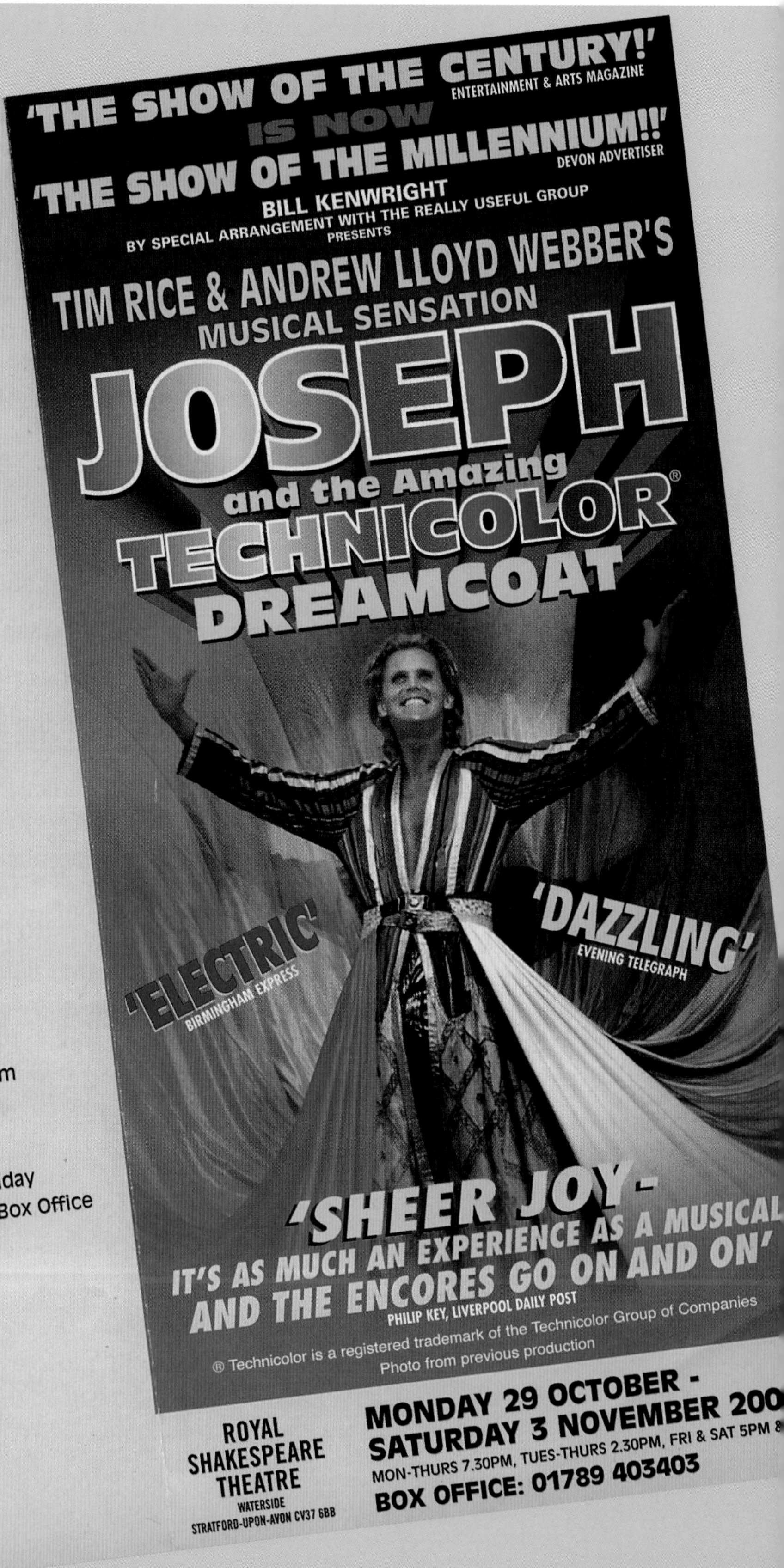
'THE SHOW OF THE CENTURY!'
ENTERTAINMENT & ARTS MAGAZINE
IS NOW
'THE SHOW OF THE MILLENNIUM!!'
DEVON ADVERTISER
BILL KENWRIGHT
BY SPECIAL ARRANGEMENT WITH THE REALLY USEFUL GROUP
PRESENTS
TIM RICE & ANDREW LLOYD WEBBER'S
MUSICAL SENSATION
JOSEPH
and the Amazing
TECHNICOLOR®
DREAMCOAT
'ELECTRIC'
BIRMINGHAM EXPRESS
'DAZZLING'
EVENING TELEGRAPH
'SHEER JOY -
IT'S AS MUCH AN EXPERIENCE AS A MUSICAL
AND THE ENCORES GO ON AND ON'
PHILIP KEY, LIVERPOOL DAILY POST
® Technicolor is a registered trademark of the Technicolor Group of Companies
Photo from previous production
ROYAL SHAKESPEARE THEATRE
WATERSIDE
STRATFORD-UPON-AVON CV37 6BB
MONDAY 29 OCTOBER -
SATURDAY 3 NOVEMBER 200
MON-THURS 7.30PM, TUES-THURS 2.30PM, FRI & SAT 5PM &
BOX OFFICE: 01789 403403

WRITING

Informing and persuading

The leaflet advertising '*Joseph and the Amazing Technicolor Dreamcoat*':
- **informs** people, ie it gives them information about the show
- **persuades** people, ie makes the show seem too good to miss.

Language features

Information

A well-designed leaflet will:
- make it clear what is being advertised

- the cost

TICKET PRICES
Monday-Thursday Evenings 7.30pm:
£20.50, £15.50, £10.00
Tuesday-Thursday Matinees 2.30pm
& Friday Matinee 5.00pm: £14.50, £10.00
Friday Evening 8.00pm, Saturday Matinee 5.00pm
& Evening 8.00pm: £22.50, £17.50, £12.00
DISCOUNTS
School Groups of 12 or more: £8.00 Monday-Friday
For other concessions available please contact the Box Office

- where and when the event is taking place.

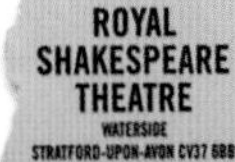

MONDAY 29 OCTOBER -
SATURDAY 3 NOVEMBER 2001
MON-THURS 7.30PM, TUES-THURS 2.30PM, FRI & SAT 5PM & 8PM
BOX OFFICE: 01789 403403

Persuasive language

Leaflets are usually a form of advertising. They use exaggerated language to grab the reader's attention, eg The show isn't just good it's:

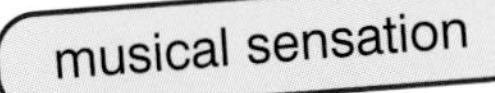

sheer joy

DAZZLING

Other people's opinions are used to persuade you to go and see the show.

What it looks like

The leaflet makes people want to read it by using:
- lots of colour
- capital letters
- different fonts and type sizes
- photographs.

Writing assignment

Design a leaflet for a play or musical event that you could put on at school. The example on the left will give you some ideas.

Remember to:
- make it eye-catching by using colour and different types of lettering
- use exaggerated language to show just how good it is going to be.

Treading the boards...

THEATRES THROUGH THE AGES

People in nearly every country and in every age have performed plays. But not every 'stage' looks the same.

Amphitheatre ▶

The Ancient Greeks and the Romans first used this type of stage outdoors to put on plays for festivals. The stage itself is round or curved and the seats for the audience are curved around the stage. Amphitheatres nowadays can be outdoors or indoors.

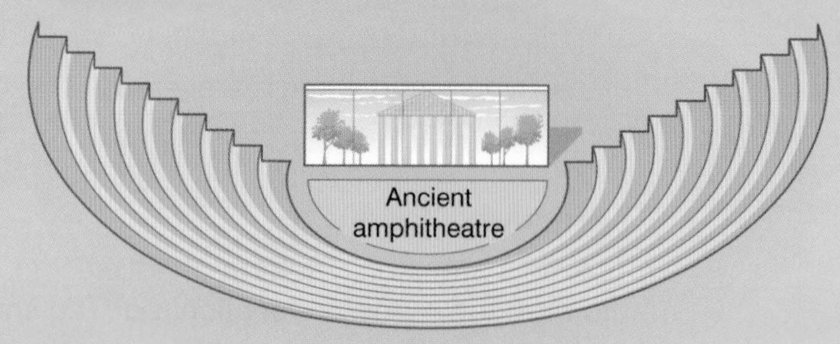

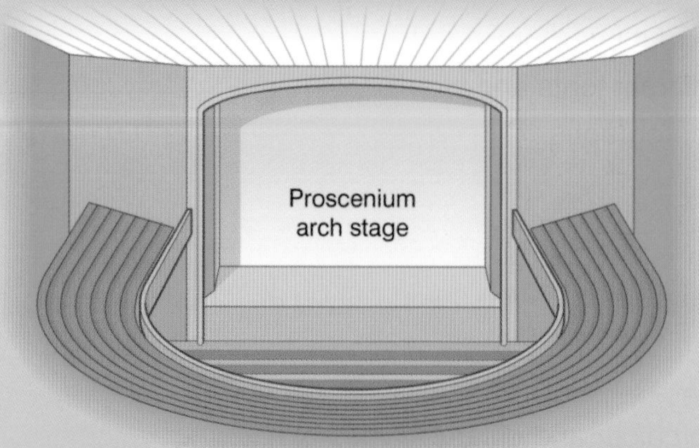

◀ Proscenium arch stage

The stage is on a raised platform. The audience is looking at the play through a 'picture frame' which is called the proscenium arch. There are curtains which can be raised and lowered, or pulled across the stage. The audience is separate from the actors. Sometimes they are even further away as there is an orchestra pit between the stage and the seats.

Thrust or apron stage ▶

This type of stage is like a Proscenium Arch stage but it comes further out into the audience. The 'apron' is the part of the stage which is not covered when the curtains close. This apron can be extended using rostra blocks so the audience can be seated on three sides of the stage. People watching the play are much closer to the actors.

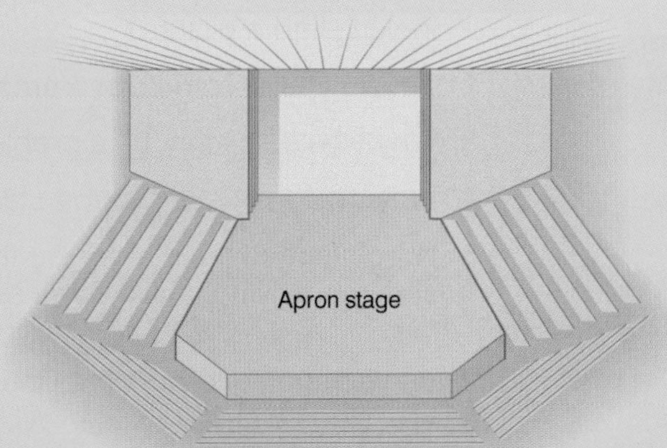

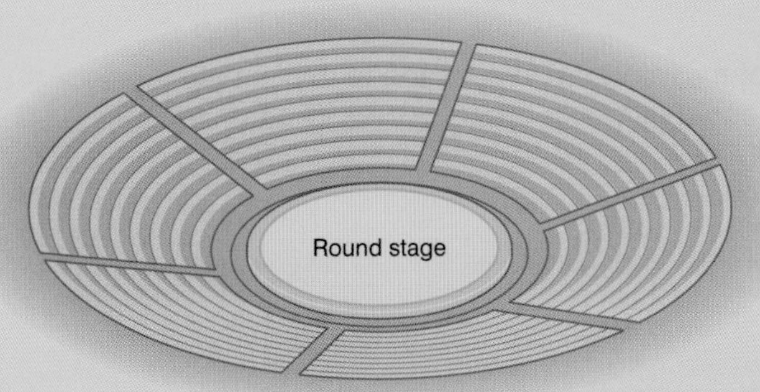

◀ Theatre-in-the-round

In this type of theatre, the stage is encircled by the audience. The actors are seen from all angles and the audience is much closer to what is going on. Obviously, there cannot be any huge scenery which would obscure the audience's view.

Lecture-style stage ▶

This is a very modern form of staging. It does not have a proscenium arch, just a flat wall behind the actors. The audience sits on tiered seating in front of the stage. The first row of seating is on the same level as the acting space. This gives the actors and audience the feeling of being in the same 'room'.

COMPREHENSION

A Write 'true' or 'false' for each of these statements.

1. The audience looks through a 'picture frame' in an amphitheatre.
2. The orchestra pit is usually placed between the stage and the audience.
3. Another name for an apron stage is a thrust stage.
4. Large pieces of scenery can be used in theatre-in-the-round.
5. A lecture-style theatre has no proscenium arch.

B **1** How does the orchestra pit add to the feeling that the audience is looking into a picture?

2 Which type of stage can a proscenium arch easily be turned into?

3 Why would scenery be a problem on a theatre-in-the-round stage?

4 Why do you think an apron stage is also known as a 'thrust' stage?

5 Which type of theatre do you think would be most suitable for someone giving a talk with a slide show?

C If you were going to put on a Christmas pantomime for families, which type of stage would you use. Why?

VOCABULARY

Use a dictionary and the context of the information passage to explain the meaning of these words. They are underlined in the passage. The first one is done for you.

1 festivals = *celebrations* **2** orchestra pit **3** rostra

4 encircled **5** obscure **6** tiered

SPELLING

Contractions

Remember! A **contraction** is used in place of two words. A letter or letters are left out and an apostrophe is used in their place,

eg they **a**re = *they're* (**a** missed out)

what **i**s = *what's* (**i** missed out)

A Write each of these contractions as two words. The first one has been done for you.

1 it's = *it is* **2** he'll **3** could've

4 mustn't **5** they've **6** I'll

7 she's **8** won't **9** we've

HINT

To contract means to shorten.

B Write each of these pairs of words as a contraction. The first one has been done for you.

1 should have = *should've* **2** we had **3** you will

4 have not **5** we are **6** did not

7 I am **8** I have **9** he is

GRAMMAR AND PUNCTUATION

Doesn't / don't; it's / its

Doesn't is the contraction for **does not**. It is used with singular nouns and singular pronouns,

eg *This **stage doesn't** have a proscenium arch.*

*It **doesn't** have a proscenium arch.*

Don't is the contraction for **do not**. It is used with plural nouns and plural pronouns,

eg *The **curtains don't** come across the stage.*

***They don't** come across the stage.*

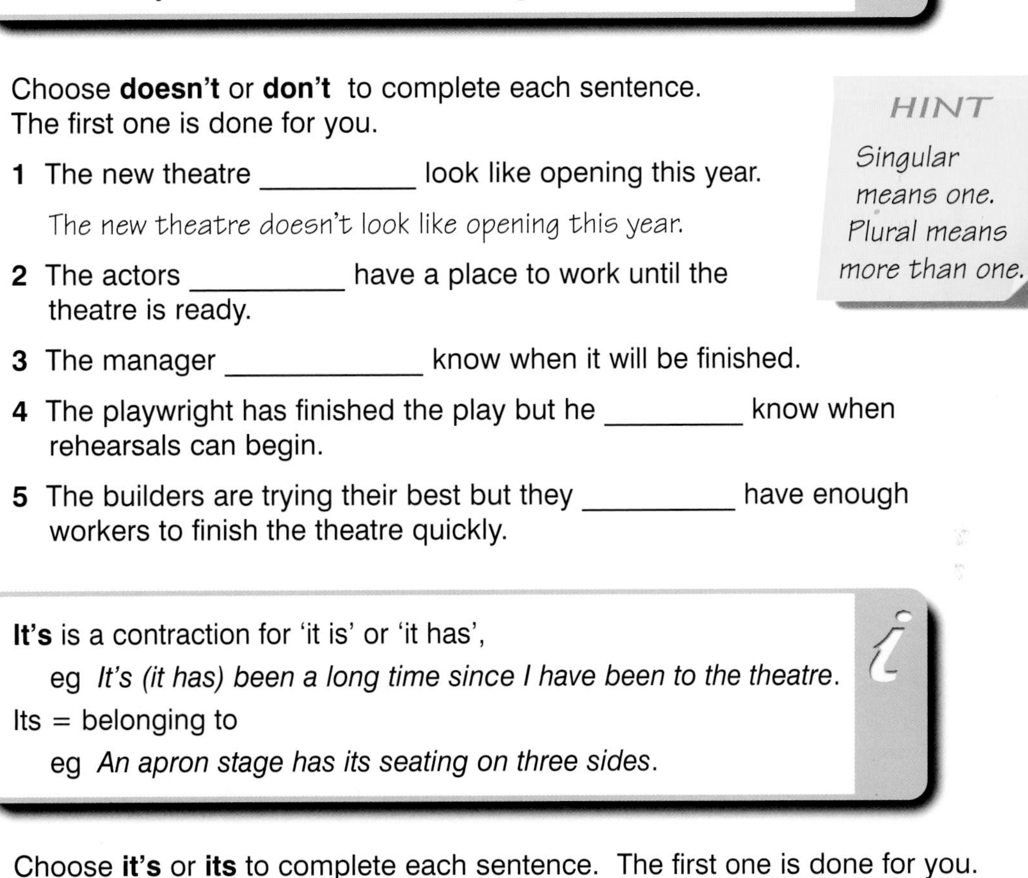

A Choose **doesn't** or **don't** to complete each sentence. The first one is done for you.

HINT

Singular means one. Plural means more than one.

1 The new theatre __________ look like opening this year.

The new theatre doesn't look like opening this year.

2 The actors __________ have a place to work until the theatre is ready.

3 The manager ____________ know when it will be finished.

4 The playwright has finished the play but he _________ know when rehearsals can begin.

5 The builders are trying their best but they __________ have enough workers to finish the theatre quickly.

It's is a contraction for 'it is' or 'it has',

eg *It's (it has) been a long time since I have been to the theatre.*

Its = belonging to

eg *An apron stage has its seating on three sides.*

B Choose **it's** or **its** to complete each sentence. The first one is done for you.

1 The new play opened last week and ______ got great reviews.

The new play opened last week and it's got great reviews.

2 The town is expanding quickly and _______ theatre is very popular.

3 No one thought that the play was very good but _____ been running for a year.

4 The theatre was very old and ______ curtains were torn and shabby.

5 Some people did not like the new theatre because ________ design was very modern.

EURIPIDES
ARISTOPHANES
SOPHOCLES

WRITING

Presenting information

The extract about different types of stages is an **information** text. It uses text and drawings so the reader can see what is being written about.

Language features

Main heading

This tells readers exactly what the information text is about:

Theatres through the ages

Sub-headings

These are used to divide up the information so that the reader can concentrate on one thing at a time, eg

Proscenium arch stage ***Theatre-in-the-round***

Style

Information texts should be written in a formal style not a 'chatty' one. A formal style:

- often uses the passive voice,
  eg '*the stage is encircled by the audience*'
- does not use contractions,
  eg '*... what is going on*' **not** '*what's*'
- uses special vocabulary to do with the subject,
  eg '*proscenium arch*', '*rostra*'
- the text is fact not opinion,
  eg '*This is a very modern form of staging*' **not** 'I don't like this modern form of staging.'

Organisation

The information is organised so that we read about one type of theatre then move on to the next one. This makes it easy for the reader to understand.

Writing assignment

There were many famous Ancient Greek playwrights. Here are three of them:

- Euripides
- Aristophanes
- Sophocles.

Research these playwrights and write an information text about them. Find out:

- when they were born and when they died
- where they lived
- the names of their plays.

Think of a main heading. Use their names as sub-headings.

Here come the clowns...

A clown's make-up

You will need:

- *clown white or cream make-up*
- *black pencil*
- *thin white liner pencil*
- *white talcum powder*
- *red lipstick*
- *thin black liner pencil*
- *black mascara*
- *triangular make-up sponges*
- *powder puff.*

What to do

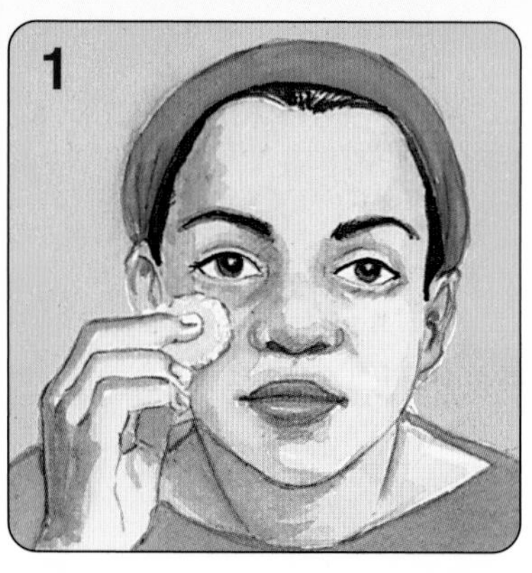

Step 1
Remove ordinary make-up and clean the face thoroughly.

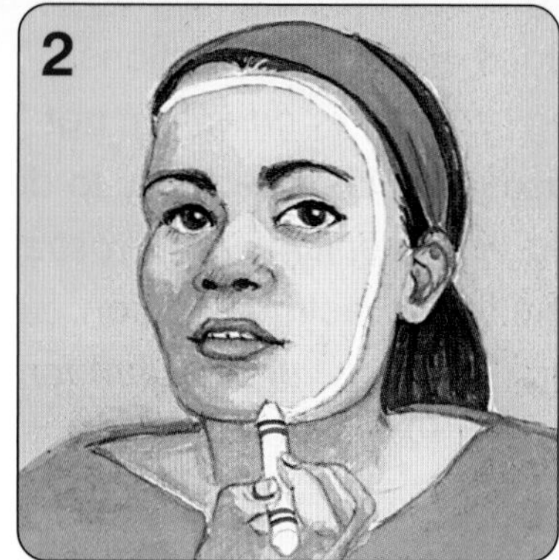

Step 2
With a white pencil, outline a 'mask' shape on the face.
Keep the line a little way from the hairline.

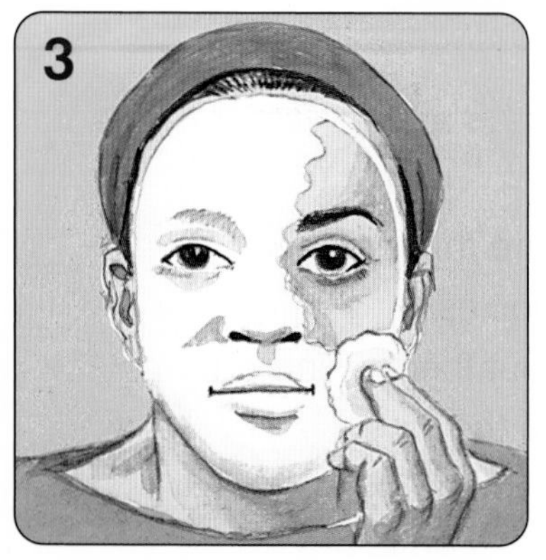

Step 3
Apply clown white make-up inside the lines with a sponge.
Apply over the eyebrows, up to the eyelashes and lips.

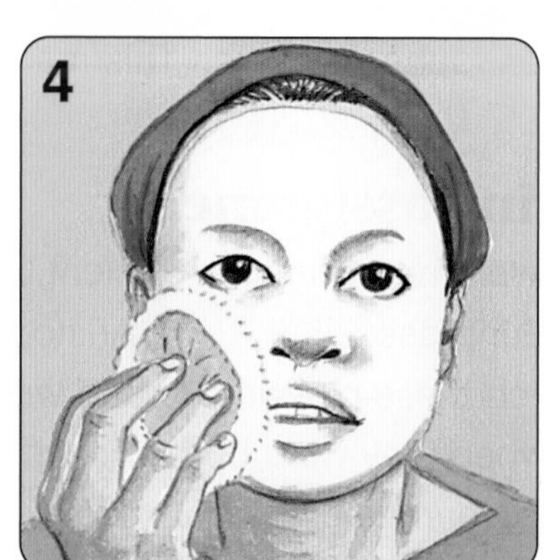

Step 4
Powder the face with a powder puff so that it is no longer sticky to the touch.

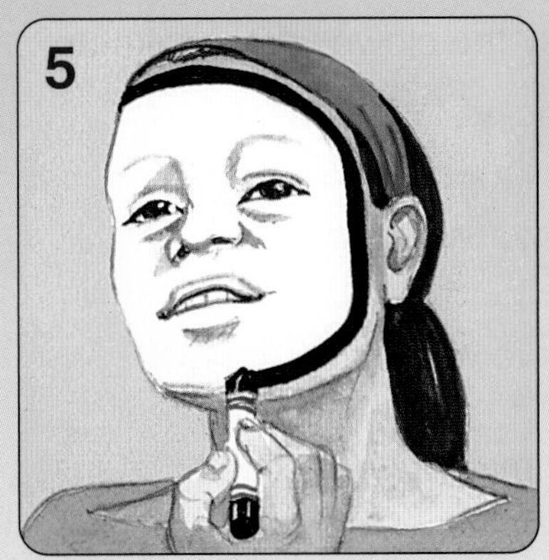

Step 5
Outline the edge of the white mask with a thick black pencil.

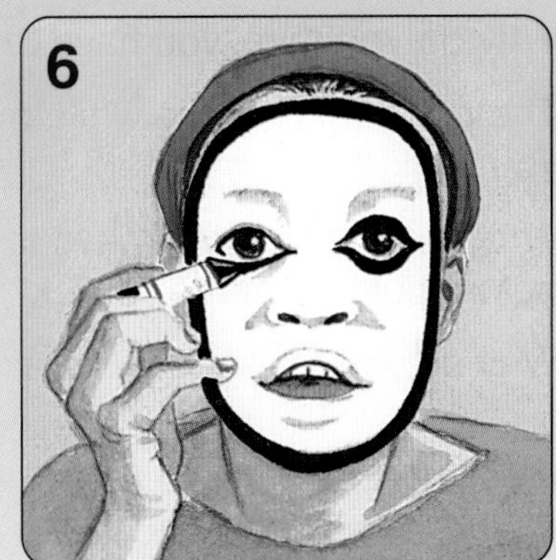

Step 6
Outline the eyes with the black liner pencil, working from the inside corner of the eye to the outside.

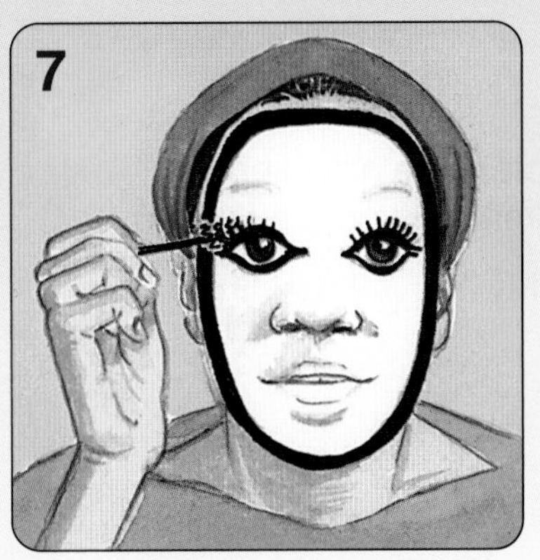

Step 7
Apply black mascara to the eyelashes.

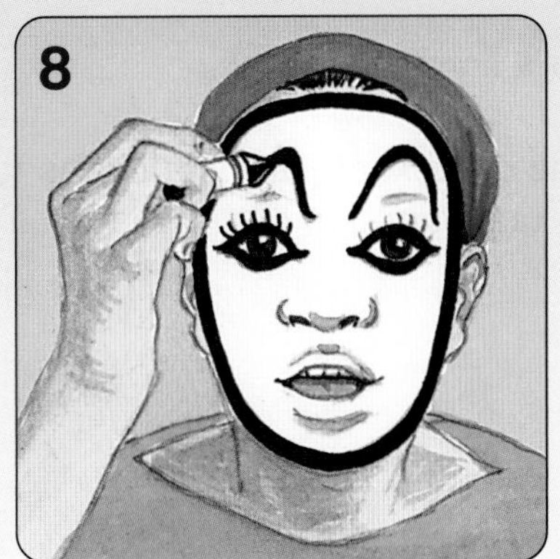

Step 8
Draw in eyebrows with a thick pencil. Put them above the real eyebrows.

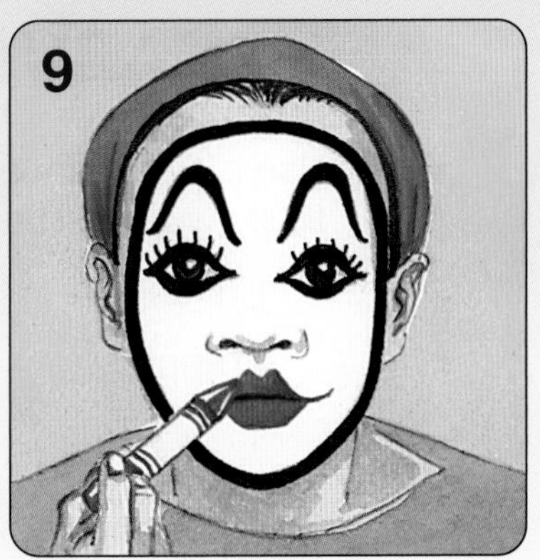

Step 9
Remove any white powder from the lips. Apply red lipstick.

COMPREHENSION

A Choose the best answer.

1. The instructions are for:
   a removing make-up **b** making up as a clown **c** how to look tanned.
2. The sponges are used for:
   a having a wash **b** applying mascara
   c applying white clown make-up.
3. Outline the edge of the white mask with:
   a a black pencil **b** a white pencil **c** red lipstick.
4. Outline the eyes in black from:
   a the top to the bottom **b** from the inside corner to the outside
   c from the outside corner to the inside.
5. The eyebrows are drawn on:
   a above real eyebrows **b** below real eyebrows **c** on real eyebrows.

B **1** Why do you think you should remove ordinary make-up first?

2 Why do you think you have to use a sponge to apply the clown white make-up?

3 The powder stops the white make-up from being '*sticky*'. Why do you think this is important?

4 Why do you think you have to '*remove any white powder from the lips*' before putting on the lipstick?

5 Why do you think clowns make themselves up to have white faces?

C Clowns use their skills to make an audience laugh, yet many people think that clowns are rather sad. Why do you think this is so?

VOCABULARY

Use a dictionary and the context of the instructions to explain the meanings of these words. They are underlined in the passage. The first one is done for you.

1 triangular = in the shape of a triangle **2** thoroughly **3** hairline

4 apply **5** outline **6** remove

SPELLING

Apostrophes of possession (plural)

Apostrophes are used to show who owns something,
eg *The **clown's** make-up was white.*
For plural nouns which usually end in **s** we just put the apostrophe after the **s**,
eg *The **clowns'** costumes were damaged.*

A Rewrite these phrases using apostrophes. The first one is done for you.

1 the white faces of the clowns = the clowns' white faces

2 the black lines of the make-up pencil **3** the outlines of the white mask

When a plural noun does not end in **s**, we add **'s**,
eg *the **children's** laughter*

B Rewrite these phrases in a shorter way using apostrophes. The first one is done for you.

1 the costumes of the men = the men's costume

2 the hats of the women **3** the cheese of the mice

GRAMMAR AND PUNCTUATION

Imperative sentences

Any writing which tells us what to do is usually written in **imperative sentences**. They begin with a verb and end with a full stop or exclamation mark,

eg **Apply** *clown white make-up with a sponge.*

imperative verb — full stop

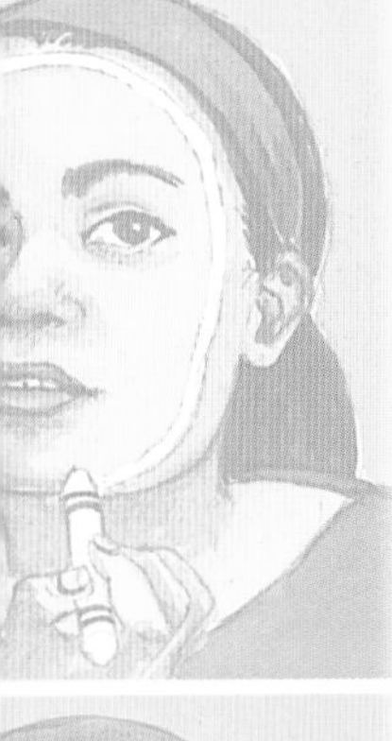

A Write these sentences as imperative sentences. The first one is done for you.

1 You should go and see the clowns.

Go and see the clowns.

2 Can you buy the tickets on your way home?

3 If you are going to be late, give me a ring.

4 You should be able to catch the last bus home.

Imperative sentences can be made negative by using 'don't' or 'never',

eg ***Laugh** at the clowns.* ***Don't laugh** at the clowns.*

***Sit** in the front row.* ***Never sit** in the front row.*

B Write these sentences as negative imperatives. The first one is done for you.

1 Put make-up on a dirty face. Never put make-up on a dirty face.

2 Come in while the clowns are performing.

3 Outline the eyes with red lipstick.

4 Use black mascara for the eyebrows.

By adding the word please, imperative sentences change from orders to **requests**,

eg *Use this lipstick.* *Use this lipstick, **please**.*

***Please** use this lipstick.*

C Write your own imperative sentences.

1 Write an imperative sentence which is an order.

2 Write an imperative sentence which is a negative imperative.

3 Write an imperative sentence as a request.

WRITING

Instructions

Here come the clowns ... is a set of **instructions**. Instructions tell us how to do something. They are written in:

- clear, short sentences
- the order in which they must be followed.

Language features

Organisation

For instructions which tell us how to do or make something, it is useful to list the equipment which is needed at the beginning,

eg *You will need: clown white or cream make-up*
black pencil

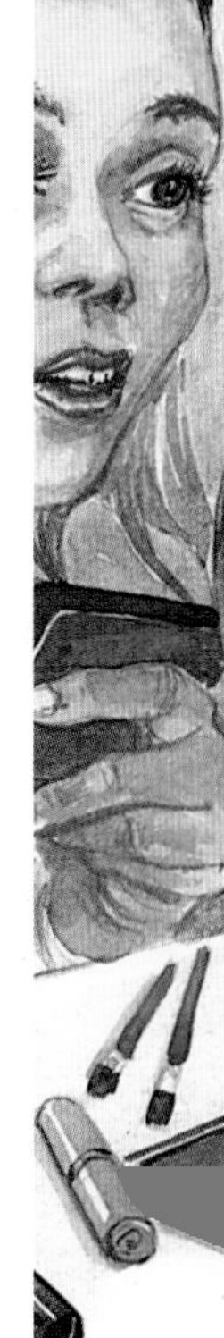

Why do you think it is a good idea to tell people what they will need at the beginning of the instructions?

Instructions should be in the order in which they should be carried out,

eg *Step 1 Remove ordinary make-up ...*
Step 2 With a white pencil ...

Why is it important to have the instructions in the correct order?

Style

Instructions must be easy to follow. You do not need long, complicated sentences which the reader might find difficult to understand.

Illustrations

Instructions are often easier to follow if each step is illustrated. You can **read** what you are supposed to do and **see** what you are supposed to do.

Imperative sentences

These sentences 'instruct' the reader what to do for the best results. Using imperative verbs means you do not have to keep repeating yourself,

eg *'Apply black mascara ...'* **not** You should apply black mascara ...
'Draw in eyebrows ...' **not** You should draw in eyebrows ...

Writing assignment

Write a set of instructions for one of the following:

- preparing a simple meal
- applying eye make-up
- cleaning football boots.

Remember to:

- list the equipment needed at the beginning
- write your instructions in the correct order
- use imperative sentences
- draw illustrations.

Published in 2005 by:
Nelson Thornes Ltd
Delta Place
27 Bath Road
CHELTENHAM
GL53 7TH
United Kingdom

09 / 10 9 8 7 6 5 4 3

A catalogue record for this book is available from the British Library

ISBN 978 0 7487 9341 9

Illustrations by Tom Barnfield, Beverly Curl, Jim Eldridge, Angela Lumley, Paul McCaffery
c/o Sylvie Poggio Artists Agency
Designed by Viners Wood Associates

Printed and bound in China by 1010 Printing International Ltd

Acknowledgements
The author and publishers wish to thank the following for permission to use copyright material and photographs in this book: David Higham Associates Ltd on behalf of the author for material from Roald Dahl, Going Solo, Jonathan Cape (1986) pp. 83, 84, 85; Bill Kenwright Ltd for material from a leaflet advertising Joseph and the Technicolor Dreamcoat; News International Newspapers Ltd for material from Denys Finch Hatton, 'An abuse of sport – stalking lion by car in the Serengeti', The Times, 21st January 1928. Copyright ©Times Newspapers Ltd, London, 1928; The New York Times Agency for material from 'Radio Listeners Panic, Taking War...', New York Times, 31st October 1938. Copyright ©1938 by the New York Times Co; Writers House LLC, agent for the proprietor, by arrangement with the Estate of Martin Luther King, Jr, for material from Martin Luther King Jr, 'I have a Dream...'. Copyright ©1963 Martin Luther King Jr, renewed copyright ©1991 Coretta Scott King.

Alfio Scigliano/Sygma/Corbis, p52; Araldo du luca/Corbis, p104; Archivo Iconografico S.A./Corbis, p104; Bettman/Corbis, p104; Carl and Ann Purcell/Corbis, p70; Corel 9 (NT), p62; Corel 13 (NT), p68; Corel 73 (NT), p74; Corel 413 (NT), p74; Corel 449 (NT), p62; Corel 640 (NT), p68; Digital Vision 14 (NT), pp52, 56; Digital Vision 15 (NT), p74; Fire Magazine, p46; Flip Schilke/Corbis, p22, 26; Imperial War Museum, p76; Mary Evans Picture Library, p16, 58, 88, 92; Natphotos/Digital Vision AF (NT), p68; Photodisc 67 (NT), p38; Rubberwall WW (NT), p38; Still Pictures, p64.

Every effort has been made to trace the copyright holders but if any have been inadvertently overlooked the publishers will be pleased to make the necessary arrangement at the first opportunity.

Biking

Rennay Craats

AV2

www.openlightbox.com

Step 1
Go to **www.openlightbox.com**

Step 2
Enter this unique code
BLWTR9CDZ

Step 3
Explore your interactive eBook!

AV2 is optimized for use on any device

Your interactive eBook comes with...

Contents
Browse a live contents page to easily navigate through resources

Audio
Listen to sections of the book read aloud

Videos
Watch informative video clips

Weblinks
Gain additional information for research

Slideshows
View images and captions

Try This!
Complete activities and hands-on experiments

Key Words
Study vocabulary, and complete a matching word activity

Quizzes
Test your knowledge

Share
Share titles within your Learning Management System (LMS) or Library Circulation System

Citation
Create bibliographical references following the Chicago Manual of Style

This title is part of our AV2 digital subscription

1-Year Grades K–5 Subscription
ISBN 978-1-7911-3320-7

Access hundreds of AV2 titles with our digital subscription.
Sign up for a FREE trial at www.openlightbox.com/trial

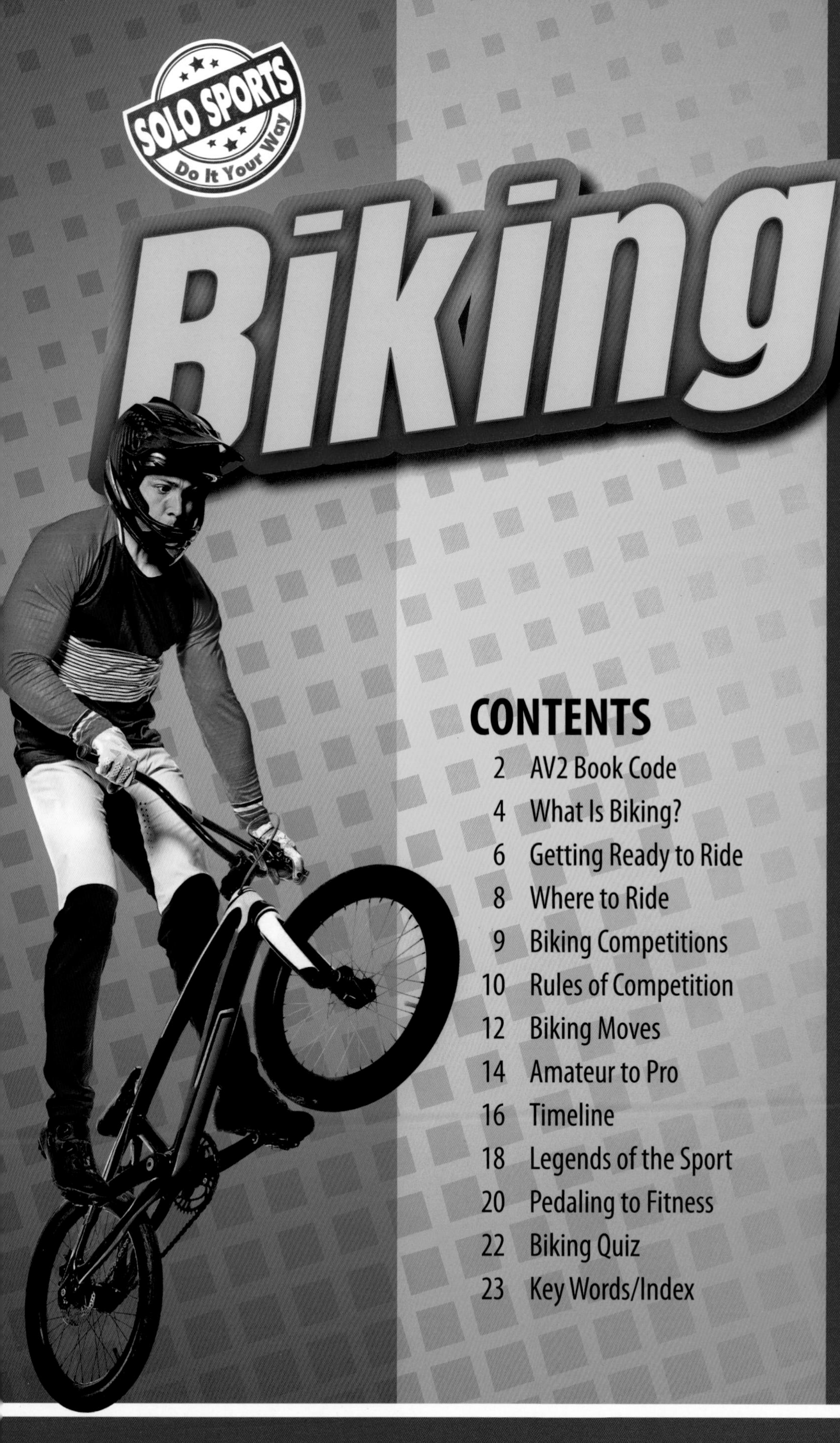

Biking

CONTENTS

What Is Biking?

People have been riding bicycles for about 200 years. As technology improved, bicycles became more advanced. By the 1960s, cycling was a popular activity for children as well as adults. With the new gearshift, riders were able to cycle off-road, but thin tires made it difficult in some areas. Many riders wanted to explore **rugged** areas on their bicycles. BMX bicycles were soon created. These low, thick-tired bicycles could withstand any **terrain**, but they were not very good for climbing hills because they only had one gear. In the 1970s, a group of cyclists in California began taking parts from one bicycle and adding them to parts of others. They used lighter materials and added many gears. The mountain bike was born.

The "Ordinary" bicycle was first produced in 1871. It had a large front wheel.

By 1983, companies across the country were making mountain bikes based on the California models. Today, mountain bikers can cycle on city streets as well as challenging mountain trails. Mountain bikes are made to absorb the shock of riding over bumpy terrain. As the slopes become steeper, bikers gear down to make pedaling easier. Some cyclists ride their bicycles to school or work rather than driving or taking public transit. They may never take their mountain bikes off paved roads or trails. Other cyclists want to discover nature. They enjoy taking their bicycles off-road, riding over rocks and through forests. Some mountain bikers enter off-road competitions and compete in cross-country or downhill races. Mountain bikes have made cycling an entirely different sport.

Cycling first became popular after the invention of the air-filled tire in 1888. Tires help to give a smoother ride when cycling over rough ground.

About **100 million bicycles** are produced around the world every year.

More than **1 billion bicycles** are in use across the globe.

Roughly **40 million people** in the United States go **mountain biking** each year.

Getting Ready to Ride

To participate in mountain biking, some basic equipment is needed. The sport can be dangerous, so riders need to take **precautions**. Proper safety gear may help prevent injuries. With the right equipment and training, mountain bikers can ride faster and farther.

The bicycle itself is the most important piece of equipment. Most mountain bikes are made from light metals, such as aluminum and **titanium**, or carbon fiber. Mountain bikes weigh from 20 to 28 pounds (9 to 13 kilograms), while road-racing bikes weigh from 16 to 20 pounds (7 to 9 kg).

Wheels on a mountain bike are relatively small to keep mountain bikers close to the ground for better control and stability. The tires on mountain bike wheels are wider than road-racing tires and have more space between **treads**. More of the tire touches the ground for better **traction**.

A helmet is needed to keep riders safe. It should fit snugly and be comfortable to wear.

Sunglasses protect riders' eyes from the harmful effects of the Sun. They also protect the eyes from dust or other particles that can be flicked up while cycling.

Serious bikers wear tight-fitting clothing. The clothes are often made from stretchy materials, such as nylon and Lycra. Less serious mountain bikers usually wear street clothes, such as T-shirts and comfortable shorts or sweat pants.

Mountain bike handlebars are straight so that riders sit upright. This allows them to see the trail ahead. To stop, riders squeeze the brake levers on the handlebars.

The bicycle chain fits along the teeth of the chainring, which is connected to the pedals. It goes around a piece called the freewheel. This is attached to the back tire. As riders pedal, the chain moves the freewheel and the tire spins.

Where to Ride

Mountain bikers are limited only by their imagination. They can ride almost anywhere. Many mountain bikers choose to ride on city trails and streets. They must obey the rules of the road, just as vehicles do. They also need to ride responsibly on trails, as many other people walk, cycle, or inline skate on these paths. There are also national parks for mountain bikers to enjoy. These areas offer bikers a chance to ride off-road in natural areas. There are often hikers or horseback riders sharing the trails. Cyclists need to be considerate of these people by giving them the right of way and riding with control.

Depending on where cyclists live, they may have the opportunity to try different kinds of mountain biking. Some adventurous riders enjoy winter riding. Snowy trails provide a challenging workout. Riders must make sure they dress in layers to stay warm. Other riders prefer the challenge of sandy areas, or dunes. Still others like to tackle the steepest hills they can find. Some ski hills allow bikers to ride the slopes in the summer. Mountain biking can take riders nearly anywhere they want to pedal. Riders need to be sure that the area is not private property or a no-cycling zone before setting out.

Warm clothing and gloves make a ride in the snow more enjoyable.

Biking Competitions

Biking competitions bring talented riders together, letting them test their skills on a variety of trails. One major competition is the Union Cycliste Internationale (UCI) Mountain Bike World Cup. It was first held in 1991. This event includes both cross-country and downhill mountain bike races.

Snowshoe, West Virginia

The Snowshoe Mountain Resort in Snowshoe, West Virginia, hosted the final round of the UCI Mountain Bike World Cup in 2019 and 2021. The Snowshoe Bike Park features close to 40 trails. It has one of the largest trail systems in eastern United States.

Rules of Competition

Different rules govern different types of mountain biking events. In the observed trials, riders make their way through a course filled with obstacles. It takes balance and control to win this event. Riders aim to finish the course with the lowest number of penalties as possible. A score of zero is a perfect ride.

Cross-country racing involves climbing steep hills and racing down them as well. Many riders compete at the same time, so riders need to race safely. Pushing or leaning on other riders during a race can result in penalties. Riders must stay on the track. Any rider who tries to take a shortcut is **disqualified**.

Some cross-country mountain bike races last about two hours. Others may last 24 hours.

For riders who want the thrill of speed, downhill racing is a great event. The only rule in this competition is to be quick. Downhill racers pedal down a dirt track, and the first to finish wins.

The dual slalom is another racing event. This competition requires two cyclists to ride through two identical courses at the same time. The course has several gates that riders must pedal through. Riders are penalized if they miss any of the markers. The cyclist who rides around all the markers and crosses the finish line first wins the race.

Riders should regularly check their tire pressure, or the amount of air in a tire, to make sure it is not too low.

Biking Moves

Many people learn to ride a bicycle when they are young. Riding a mountain bike involves some extra skills. Turning, for example, requires more than just moving the handlebars. Riders need to lean in the direction they are turning. The sharper the turn or the faster they ride, the more they need to lean.

Fast riding means cyclists also need to know how to stop. The left brake controls the front brake, and the right brake controls the back brake. To stay balanced, riders lean back and keep their bodies low while braking.

Experience teaches cyclists when to use which gears. Lower gears allow riders to pedal faster. This makes it easier to climb steep hills. Higher gears make for tougher pedaling. These are used for control when traveling downhill. Cyclists must be pedaling when changing gears. Riders must also learn to shift their weight to make uphill or downhill cycling easier.

On long climbs, riders use lower gears and move their weight forward.

Some areas are too tough to ride through. Riders must pick up their bikes and carry them to easier terrain. To do this, riders often put one arm under the top bar and rest the bicycle on their shoulder. Then, they hold the handlebars to keep them steady, and stand to lift the bike. The free hand is used to move obstacles, such as branches, out of the way, and for balance.

Riders also need to learn to avoid obstacles. To do this, they steer toward the obstacle at first and then quickly lean to one side to move around the obstacle. Other riders choose to go over obstacles rather than around them. This is called log-hopping. Cyclists log-hop by riding quickly and then leaning back while pulling the front wheel off the ground. When the back wheel is about to contact the obstacle, riders shift their weight forward, drawing the back wheel up. To cross ditches, cyclists ride into the ditch at an angle. As they come out of the ditch, they lean back and keep their bodies low on the bike.

The front brakes are stronger than the back brakes. A rider risks falling forward off the bike if he or she uses only the front brakes when biking downhill.

Carrying a mountain bike through rough terrain is hard work, so it is only done for short distances.

Amateur to Pro

Many cyclists begin mountain biking as a hobby. People of all ages can enjoy a bike ride. Other cyclists use biking as a way to get where they need to be. For those cyclists who enjoy the challenge of competition, there are many contests and races to enter on mountain bikes, BMX bikes, or road-racing bikes.

Athletes can compete in downhill, uphill, or cross-country races. Other contests require cyclists to ride through a course full of obstacles. All of these events challenge the **endurance** and strength of the rider.

Mountain bikes are one of the most popular bikes in the United States. About 25 percent of all bikes in the country are mountain bikes.

The world's longest mountain bike race is the Tour Divide. It takes place on the 2,750-mile (4,400-km) long Great Divide trail. The trail begins in Alberta, Canada, and ends in Antelope Wells, New Mexico.

In 1920, the Amateur Bicycle League of America was created. It was renamed USA Cycling in 1995. The group now has more than 60,000 members. It hosts the USA Cycling Mountain Bike National Championships.

As mountain bikers improve and win competitions, they may decide to try out for regional or national teams. Many work to earn a place on the Olympic team. The Olympics offer several different categories for cycling. Some cyclists compete in road races or on tracks.

Mountain bikers compete in the cross-country event. The race can take competitors across fields, and along forest roads and paths. Riders might race from one point to another, or be required to complete multiple laps of the same course. The first rider across the finish line claims the gold medal. After taking part in the Olympics, mountain bikers and other riders can attract **sponsorship** and compete professionally around the world.

BMX racing is a popular sport. "BMX" stands for bicycle motocross. Riders copy many tricks from gas-powered dirt-bike riders.

BMX bicycles are low to the ground and have thick tires. They are sturdy enough to survive the sport's rough landings.

Timeline

As bicycles have evolved from their humble beginnings, so has the sport of cycling. Mountain biking and BMX racing competitions are especially popular today. Many mountain bikers were trained in BMX racing.

BMX races can take place indoors or outside. Hills and dips are built into the course as obstacles. Riders race around sharp corners and over challenging jumps.

1817 Baron Karl von Drais builds the velocipede. This bike-like device has two wheels. It is propelled by the rider pushing off the ground with his or her feet.

1863 People in Paris, France, improve upon the velocipede by adding pedals.

1977 Joe Breeze builds and sells the "Breezer," one of the first modern mountain bikes.

1996 Mountain biking debuts as an Olympic sport in Atlanta, Georgia.

2019 BMX rider Ryan Williams wins his third **X Games** gold medal in Minneapolis, Minnesota, for the BMX Big Air Event.

2021 Hannah Roberts wins the silver medal for Team USA at the Olympics in Tokyo, Japan. She competes in the women's BMX freestyle event.

*BMX events were included in the **first X Games**, which was held in **1995**.*

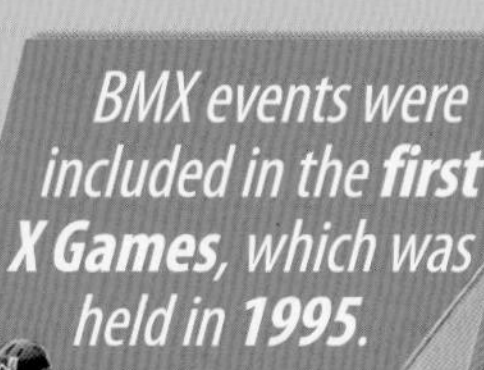

*BMX biking became an **Olympic sport** in **2008** at the Beijing Summer Olympics.*

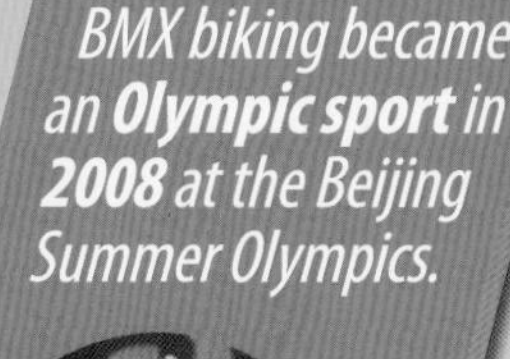

*The **dirt tracks** BMX riders race on are usually **700 to 1,300 feet** (200 to 400 meters) long.*

Legends of the Sport

Biking superstars have helped make the sport more popular.

David "Tinker" Juarez

BIRTH DATE: March 4, 1961
HOMETOWN: Los Angeles, California, United States

CAREER FACTS:

- David was originally a BMX racer. He started cycling in 1986.
- In 1995, David won a gold medal at the Pan American Games.
- David was a three-time national cross-country champion. He was ranked number one overall in the senior men's category on the professional men's World Cup circuit.
- Many people know David as "Tinker." He got the nickname as a young boy, and it stuck.
- David was a member of the 1996 and 2000 U.S. Olympic cycling teams.

Paola Pezzo

BIRTH DATE: January 8, 1969
HOMETOWN: Verona, Italy

CAREER FACTS:

- Paola started cycling in 1989.
- In 1997, Paola won the World XC MTB Championships and the World Cup.
- Paola once rode 93 miles without stopping.
- In 1996, Paola won a gold medal in cross-country mountain biking at the Olympic Games. She defended her title and won the gold again at the Sydney Olympics in 2000.
- Paola competed in the Olympics one last time in 2004.

Alison Dunlap

BIRTH DATE: July 27, 1969
HOMETOWN: Colorado Springs, Colorado, United States

CAREER FACTS:

- Alison began cycling when she was 19 years old.
- In 1994, Alison separated her shoulder and broke three teeth in a crash, but returned to competing after she recovered.
- Alison competed in the 1996 and 2000 Olympic Games.
- In 2000, Alison won both the USCF National Cyclocross championships and the SuperCup Cyclocross Series.
- Alison was the top U.S. rider at the 2000 World Mountain Bike Championships in Spain.

Justin Williams

BIRTH DATE: May 26, 1989
HOMETOWN: Los Angeles, California, United States

CAREER FACTS:

- Justin became a professional cyclist at the age of 17.
- Justin's father and uncle were both cyclists in Belize, which inspired him to take up the sport.
- Justin won the junior U.S. national title for track racing three years in a row, in 2006, 2007, and 2008.
- In 2015 and 2018, Justin and his brother, Cory, won the Holy Saturday race in Belize as a two-person team.
- In 2019, Justin and Cory formed the L39ION racing team. Its goal is to increase diversity and inclusion within the cycling community.

Pedaling to Fitness

Cycling is a demanding sport. It takes energy and endurance to ride a bike. Riders need to eat the right foods to keep their bodies fit for the challenge. A diet rich in vegetables, fruits, meats, breads and cereals, and milk and milk products is a great way to stay healthy. These tasty and nutritious foods provide bikers with important vitamins, minerals, protein, and fiber to keep their bodies at their best. Cyclists should also keep a water bottle with them on rides so that they can stay **hydrated**. They need to replace the water they lose through sweating while exercising.

Cyclists should start drinking water 72 hours before a race to ensure that they are properly hydrated.

Most fruits and vegetables are naturally low in fat and provide many nutrients important for health.

Riders also need to keep their muscles in shape. Before hopping onto a mountain bike, riders should do a short warmup and then stretch well. Leg stretches, such as lunges and V-sits, are especially useful for cyclists. Keeping leg muscles supple helps prevent strains and injuries. Even after stretching well, riders do not start pedaling hard and fast. They begin slowly to get their bodies ready for action. During the winter, some cyclists visit their local gym and use the exercise bikes or other machines to keep fit.

Riding with friends is a great way to swap tips on how to look after a bike. It also gives riders the chance to try out other bikes.

- 1 -

How do **sunglasses** protect bike riders?

- 2 -

When was the **UCI Mountain Bike World Cup** first held?

- 3 -

What does **"BMX"** stand for?

- 4 -

Which early mountain bike did **Joe Breeze** build and sell in **1977**?

BIKING QUIZ

- 5 -

By what nickname do many people know **David Juarez**?

- 6 -

How much do mountain bikes **weigh**?

- 7 -

When did BMX biking become an **Olympic sport**?

- 8 -

What **materials** are most mountain bikes made from?

- 9 -

Which bicycle with a **large front wheel** was first produced in **1871**?

- 10 -

What is it called when a rider chooses to **go over an obstacle** rather than around it?

ANSWERS: **1** By protecting riders' eyes from the harmful effects of the Sun and from dust or other particles that can be flicked up while cycling **2** 1991 **3** Bicycle motocross **4** The "Breezer" **5** "Tinker" **6** 20 to 28 pounds (9 to 13 kg) **7** 2008 **8** Light metals, such as aluminum and titanium, or carbon fiber **9** The "Ordinary" bicycle **10** Log-hopping

Key Words

disqualified: not allowed to compete in a contest after breaking the rules

endurance: ability to survive hardship

hydrated: having enough water in the body to keep it functioning correctly

precautions: safety measures

rugged: having a rough, uneven surface

sponsorship: money or products from a corporation or individual to fund an athlete

terrain: natural features of a stretch of land

titanium: a light, strong, silver-gray metal

traction: grip

treads: patterns in a tire for gripping

X Games: a popular extreme sports competition that includes events in BMX riding, skateboarding, snowboarding, and more

Index

Get the best of both worlds.

AV2 bridges the gap between print and digital.

The expandable resources toolbar enables quick access to content including **videos**, **audio**, **activities**, **weblinks**, **slideshows**, **quizzes**, and **key words**.

Animated videos make static images come alive.

Resource icons on each page help readers to further **explore key concepts**.

Published by Lightbox Learning Inc.
276 5th Avenue, Suite 704 #917
New York, NY 10001
Website: www.openlightbox.com

Library of Congress Cataloging-in-Publication Data available upon request.

ISBN 978-1-7911-4583-5 (hardcover)
ISBN 978-1-7911-4584-2 (softcover)
ISBN 978-1-7911-4585-9 (multi-user eBook)

Printed in Guangzhou, China
1 2 3 4 5 6 7 8 9 0 26 25 24 23 22

032022
101121

Project Coordinator Priyanka Das
Designer Terry Paulhus

Photo Credits
Every reasonable effort has been made to trace ownership and to obtain permission to reprint copyright material. The publisher would be pleased to have any errors or omissions brought to its attention so that they may be corrected in subsequent printings. The publisher acknowledges Alamy, Bridgeman Images, Getty Images, and Shutterstock as its primary image suppliers for this title.